ONE WEEK LOAN

Countryside Recreation

Other titles from E & FN Spon

Amenity Landscape Management: A resources handbook
R. Cobham

Countryside Conservation
Second edition
B. Green

Countryside Management
P. Bromley

Ecology and Management of Coppice Woodlands
G. P. Buckley

The Ecology of Urban Habitats
O.L. Gilbert

Environmental Planning for Site Development
A. R. Beer

Fungal Diseases of Amenity Turf Grasses
Third edition
J. Drew Smith, N. Jackson and A. R. Woolhouse

The Golf Course: Planning, design, construction and management
F. W. Hawtree

Grounds Maintenance: A contractor's guide to competitive tendering
P. Sayers

Leisure and Recreation Management
Second edition
G. Torkildsen

Managing Sport and Leisure Facilities: A guide to competitive tendering
P. Sayers

Project Management Demystified: Today's tools and techniques
G. Reiss

Spon's Grounds Maintenance Contract Handbook
R. M. Chadwick

Spon's Landscape Contract Manual
H. Clamp

Spon's Landscape and External Works Price Book
Derek Lovejoy & Partners and Davis Langdon & Everest

Tree Form, Size and Colour: A guide to selection, planning and design
B. Gruffydd

Effective Speaking: Communicating in speech
C. Turk

Effective Writing: Improving scientific, technical and business communication
Second edition
C. Turk and J. Kirkman

Good Style: Writing for science and technology
J. Kirkman

Writing Successfully in Science
M. O'Connor

Journals

International Play Journal
Edited by B. Hughes

Leisure Studies
Edited by J. Long, M. Talbot and F. Coalter

For more information on these and other titles please contact:
The Promotion Department, E & FN Spon, 2–6 Boundary Row,
London SE1 8HN. Telephone 071–865 0066.

Countryside Recreation

A handbook for managers

Peter Bromley

Executive Director
Creswell Groundwork Trust
Whaley Thorns Heritage Centre
Nottinghamshire
UK

E & FN SPON

An Imprint of Chapman & Hall

London · Glasgow · New York · Tokyo · Melbourne · Madras

Published by E & FN Spon, an imprint of Chapman & Hall, 2–6 Boundary Row, London SE1 8HN

Chapman & Hall, 2–6 Boundary Row, London SE1 8HN, UK

Blackie Academic & Professional, Wester Cleddens Road, Bishopbriggs, Glasgow G64 2NZ, UK

Chapman & Hall Inc., One Penn Plaza, 41st Floor, New York NY10119, USA

Chapman & Hall Japan, Thomson Buildings, Hirakawacho Nemoto Building, 6F, 1–7–11 Hirakawa-cho, Chiyoda-ku, Tokyo 102, Japan

Chapman & Hall Australia, Thomas Nelson Australia, 102 Dodds Street, South Melbourne, Victoria 3205, Australia

Chapman & Hall India, R. Seshadri, 32 Second Main Road, CIT East, Madras 600 035, India

First edition 1994

© 1994 Peter Bromley

Phototypeset in 10/12pt Times by Intype, London
Printed in Great Britain by The Alden Press, Oxford

ISBN 0 419 18200 4

A catalogue record for this book is available from the British Library

Library of Congress Cataloging-in-Publication data available

∞ Printed on permanent acid-free text paper, manufactured in accordance with the proposed ANSI/NISO Z 39.48–1992 and ANSI Z 39.48–1984

This book is dedicated to
Philippa, Ruth and Patrick

Contents

Preface

There are many reasons why a book might be written. This one had its genesis in a single question once asked of me early in my career. Having collected and analysed a mass of data about landscape change and public and recreational use of land, my manager asked me 'Well, what are you going to do about it?' or words to that effect.

This book, many years too late, is one response to that question. Managers operate amidst an array of information; this is no less true of countryside managers. A large number of texts already exist that provide excellent backgrounds to countryside leisure trends, and the history of countryside recreation. However, the manager is still faced with using this information and whatever information he or she collects independently. At some point, information needs to be turned into action. The manager 'needs to do something about it'.

The management of countryside recreation draws upon many strands of supportive disciplines; management, environmental conservation, leisure management and others. This book does not, therefore, intend to provide either an historic or a theoretical perspective on countryside recreation. It does seek to provide the manager and the decision maker with a mechanism for making the necessary decisions and for assessing the parameters which must guide these decisions. For this reason, the text follows the process of management in a logical way looking to each of the issues in turn. However, the text is dotted with case studies and examples that show the tactics that many use to reach their objectives. Indeed, it could be said that this variation in tactics is one of the features of countryside recreation management, but underlying the variation is a deeper commonality.

The question 'Well, what are you going to do about it?' was one of the starting points for this book. The other was my own desire to make sense of the processes that influenced my works. By doing this, I hoped not only to do my job better, but also, naïvely, to make it easier. The actual result was that, during the period of writing the book, my life became infinitely more complicated. However, if I have helped others to make better sense of some of the pressures within which they operate, then I am more than satisfied with the outcome.

Peter Bromley
September 1993

Acknowledgements

Thanks are, as usual, due to many people and organizations. First, to the people who helped me actually prepare the book; Ian for the diagrams and Mark for nearly taking the photographs!

Thanks are also due to several professional people who have encouraged me along the way: Professor A. L. Rosen of the Queens Research Unit, New York; Nick Holliday of the Countryside Commission; Julian Ringer of ERL; Jim King formerly of Shropshire County Council; and Gordon Berkley who pointed out some of my gaps last time around.

The diagrams, facts, figures, quotes, etc., are drawn from many sources which are acknowledged individually. But I must thank the numerous individuals who work in these organizations from whom I draw much enthusiasm, encouragement and enjoyment.

Finally, a really big 'thank you' to Mr and Mrs Bromley of JB Educational Services (Spanish office) and the Surrey office of JB Educational Services for their help down the years. And, of course, Gillian, without whom, none of this would have been possible, or indeed, worthwhile.

Introduction 1

Many powerful trends have been evident in Britain in the latter part of the 20th century. Two are of particular interest here. First, there has been a growing availability of 'leisure time' – the time not required for paid employment, and not spent on other requirements, such as sleeping. Indeed, almost all other activities can now be classed as leisure pursuits: eating, travelling, sports, watching television and even shopping. The leisure industry is therefore correspondingly large and diverse. Dower (1965) identified leisure as the fourth great wave to break across Britain – the previous three having been industrialization, the network of railways and the power of the car to allow personal access.

The second trend evident within Britain has been the growth in concern about, and interest in, the environment, particularly the natural environment. This has manifested itself in many ways, including growth in membership levels of environmental organizations such as The National Trust or The Royal Society for the Protection of Birds, or through political or pressure group activities by organizations like Friends of the Earth or Greenpeace or a change in emphasis of more traditional ones such as the Country Landowners Association or the National Farmers Union.

If these two strong influences of change are combined, they inevitably lead to a growth in demand for leisure or recreational access and opportunities within the natural environment. Whilst it is difficult if not impossible to measure accurately something which is by definition informal, figures that reflect levels of demand for countryside recreation do show a large increase over the last quarter of the 20th century. In 1984, it was estimated that on a warm summer Sunday up to two-fifths of the entire population of Britain are visiting the countryside. Put another way; over a four week period during the summer months, 70% of the population will visit the countryside at least once (Countryside Commission, 1985c).

Recreational pressure is only one of the demands being made upon the British countryside: land is required for agriculture, forestry, building, nature conservation and a whole range of uses. Many of their uses can be reconciled by careful planning and countryside management (Bromley, 1990). However, it is clear that, with such a large amount of demand, some sites will inevitably be required to cater primarily for countryside recreation. The intention to cater for such recreational demand may stem from a variety of causes: the wish to protect the environment, the desire, or statutory obligations, to produce a range of recreational opportunities, or the desire to make money out of an area of countryside.

In order to assess how countryside recreation sites should be developed and managed, it is, therefore, important to understand initially the main characteristics of such a site and how it fits in with the overall pattern of change in environmentalism and recreational demand.

1.1 COUNTRYSIDE RECREATION SITES

It is perhaps easiest to understand what is meant by the term 'countryside recreation site' by giving a number of examples of the type of site covered by this generic term. The commonest is perhaps the country park – a concept that came into popular use with the 1968 Countryside Act (and its counterparts in Scotland). The purpose of a country park, as defined under the relevant Acts of Parliament is to provide a site in the countryside for the purpose of 'providing or improving opportunities for the enjoyment of the countryside' (Countryside Act, 1968, section 6 (1)).

The power to provide country parks rests mainly with Local Authorities, although privately managed and/or owned country parks can be created, providing that they meet the criteria laid out in the Act. Furthermore, the country parks must also meet the standards required by the then Countryside Commission for England, or the Countryside Councils for Scotland and Wales.

The 1968 Act clearly emphasizes the recreational use of the countryside through the country parks system. As if to further emphasize this, section 6(1) of the Acts adds, that in locating a country park, the providers should have regard 'to the location of that area in the countryside in relation to an urban or built-up area'.

The 1968 Act further outlines types of provision that might be made within country parks, and specifically mentions open air recreation, sailing, boating, fishing, picnic sites and camping. Equally importantly, the Act also identifies an important prerequisite in undertaking work

Figure 1.1 Even the most wild landscapes are managed in some way.

in the countryside; namely that the natural beauty and amenity of the countryside should be protected and safeguarded.

The 1968 Act, therefore, goes a long way towards providing a clear definition of a countryside recreation site. In short, such a site provides for open air recreation (of both a 'formal' and 'informal' nature) whilst at the same time accepting that an integral part of the recreational experience is provided by the environment itself and that this must be conserved.

The country park is perhaps the most easily identifiable countryside recreation site, but others do exist: picnic sites, for example, may contain several elements characteristic of a country park, and similarly, areas of woodland or open countryside do not necessarily need the title of 'country park' to be used or managed as a countryside recreation site.

A more nebulous site might be one that is owned or managed by several individuals but through which runs a network of low-key facilities (car parks, footpaths, notice boards or picnic areas) which in total add up to a definable 'site' which can be managed as a single facility.

On a large scale, this definition might fit a National Park (or Regional Park in Scotland) and at a local level it might cover a countryside project such as the Bollin Valley in Manchester.

Whilst this type of 'site' may not be as easily conceivable as a site that is in single ownership, it is perhaps a concept that will become increasingly important. For example, in 1991, the then Secretary of State for the Environment called for 'new purposes to the function of Green Belts . . . to enhance beauty . . . and to increase the opportunities for quiet enjoyment of the countryside' (recorded in Elson, 1992).

This call is both a reflection of existing trends in patterns of countryside recreation, and a guide towards a broader based function for the countryside, not just specific or designated areas of countryside (Curry, 1991). Furthermore, as proposals for National Parks in England and Wales suggest, the balance of needs met through the parks will not only need continued, pro-active management, but the model will also need to be extended to new sites, such as the Broads, the New Forest or even to Scotland (Department of the Environment, 1992).

Finally the location of a countryside recreation site is not necessarily restricted to what might be commonly accepted as countryside. Areas in both remote, relatively wild countryside and in urban fringe, built-up areas can act equally well as sites for countryside recreation. Whilst the types of management of those two extremes will clearly be different, the underlying objectives of providing recreational opportunities and protecting the natural environment will still be relevant.

It is important at this stage to note more recent views on the role and purpose of countryside recreation sites. Whilst the individual site remains important, however, its ownership and management structure is framed, the site itself is increasingly being seen as a gateway to wider countryside recreational opportunities. For the private landowner, encouraging visitors to go off-site will not be appealing, but for local authorities, encouragement to create wider opportunities is coming from several quarters, notably the Countryside Commission. 'Today the concern for the commission is for the whole countryside' (Countryside Commission, 1991). For the purpose of the discussion here, the importance of this slowly changing vision of countryside recreation is that the function of site-specific management will broaden to encompass these wider objectives, as discussed above.

To summarize, therefore, countryside recreation sites can be one of many forms, located in a variety of types of countryside but must always seek to meet a balance between the different pressures on the countryside. Striking this balance is the job of the site manager.

1.2 MANAGING THE COUNTRYSIDE

In order to manage a countryside recreation site effectively, the manager must have at the very least an understanding of three interlinking areas of responsibility: namely, the management of the resource; management for recreation; and the management of the system (Countryside Staff Training Advisory Group, 1989).

1.2.1 Managing the resource

The site manager must understand the principles of landscape and habitat management, particularly those aspects of conservation which relate specifically to their own site. This will range from practical skills such as woodland management or footpath construction to wider concerns such as landscape policy and environmental law. Clearly, no individual can be expected to hold detailed knowledge on all of these issues, but an overall understanding is necessary. The national context of changes to the countryside is relatively well documented in Open University (1985) and Blunden and Curry (1988) for example, and practical conservation is discussed by Tait, Lane and Carr (1988).

1.2.2 Managing for people

Countryside recreation implies that the site concerned will attract, and seek to provide enjoyment for, people. The site manager must, therefore, be concerned with providing an enjoyable opportunity for the visitors. This concern will reflect thorough knowledge of access laws, marketing strategies and types of provision. The Countryside Commission (1987b) identifies the major consideration facing those managers seeking to develop countryside recreation sites, as the ability to understand and provide for people.

1.2.3 Managing the system

As well as managing the physical resource and the people visiting the recreation site, the manager must also be responsible for the economic and business environment within which the site operates. This involves a wide range of management skills such as organizational skill, staff control, budgeting, establishing office procedures and understanding business law. On its own, this aspect of management is large enough. When coupled with the previous two areas of responsibility, the breadth of understanding necessary to develop and control a countryside recreation site becomes clear. Managing the system, as defined here, is an area of expertise in itself, to which Young (1986) provides a useful introduction.

In order to balance these various issues, the manager must clearly establish priorities within the countryside recreation site, and this is usually undertaken through the site management plan. This is discussed in Chapter 3. Further chapters introduce elements of management as outlined here – financial control, legal constraints, staffing and the provision of recreational facilities are all covered within the text.

It is evident that all of the relevant issues cannot be covered in complete detail within this book, so some importance must be attached to the references which accompany each chapter.

Recreation in the countryside | 2

2.1 INTRODUCTION

The specific demand for recreational opportunities in the countryside has increased enormously over the years since 1945. More particularly, this increase in demand has become more noticeable since the 1960s, with the desire to get away from the predominantly urban environment where some 80–90% of the British population live.

This increase in demand has manifested itself in several ways. Table 2.1 for example, shows the number of visitors to ten National Parks in England and Wales in 1984. Figure 2.1 shows the relative proportion of people visiting the countryside in 1986. More recent evidence suggests that this demand has not, as yet, levelled out (Countryside Commission, 1989).

The development of the demand for countryside recreation can be traced through several stages, with major influencing factors being identified. For the most part, factors are physical or socio-economic, but the underlying psychological desire to 'get back to nature', 'find peace and quiet' or 'to just sit in a nice place' must never be underestimated. Torkildsen (1986) explores several theories which drive people's desire for recreation and leisure activity. Phrases such as 'self-discovery', 'rehabilitation', 'confidence boosting', 'fulfilment', 'fun' and 'friendship' recur often. Kraus (1978) has explored the psychological links between leisure and modern society. Whilst many of these links exist for more formal recreational opportunities (such as team games, sports or structured play) they hold equally well for people who seek informal countryside recreation.

This chapter examines the developments of demand for countryside

Table 2.1 Key statistics for National Parks, including visitor numbers

	Brecon Beacons	Dartmoor	Exmoor	Lake District	Northum-berland	North York Moors	Peak District	Pembroke-shire coast	Snowdonia	Yorkshire Dales
Designated:										
Order	10th	4th	8th	2nd	9th	6th	1st	5th	3rd	7th
Year	1957	1951	1954	1951	1956	1952	1951	1952	1951	1954
Area:										
km^2	1344	945	686	2243	1031	1432	1404	583	2171	1761
(miles^2)	(519)	(365)	(265)	(880)	(398)	(533)	(542)	(225)	(838)	(680)
Population	32 170	29 139	10 438	39 835	2219	24 599	37 368	21 531	23 761	16 842
Visitor days per annum (millions)	7	8	2.5	20	1	11	20	1.5	9	7.5

Source: Countryside Commission (1987) *National Parks: Our Manifesto*

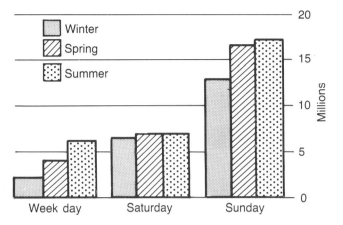

Figure 2.1 Countryside recreation trips by season and day of the week. From Countryside Commission (1985) *Household Recreation Survey.*

recreation, and presents an overview of the provision for this demand within Britain: in short, the context within which each individual site manager must operate.

2.2 AN HISTORIC PERSPECTIVE

In 1965, John Dower wrote

> Three great waves have broken across the face of Britain since 1800. First, the sudden growth of dark industrial towns. Second, the thrusting movement along far flung railways. Third, the sprawl of car-based suburbs. Now we see, under the guise of a modest word, the surge of a fourth wave which could be more powerful than all the others. The modest word is leisure.
>
> *Leisure: The fourth wave*

With this somewhat chilling assessment, Dower first expressed the growing awareness that the leisure boom was a phenomenon for which careful planning and management was required. Fieldwork and analysis undertaken within the 1960s concentrated upon the parameters that affected the demand for leisure activities in general and the types of activity for which demand was greatest.

Figure 2.2 shows projected growth from 1965 to 2000 for six of the more obvious determinants of the demand for leisure; by definition these will have a corresponding effect upon the demand for countryside

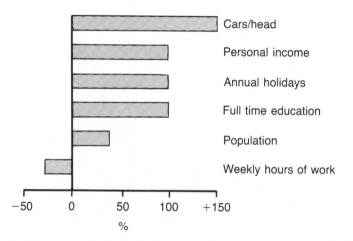

Figure 2.2 Changes in factors affecting recreation 1965–2000. From Patmore (1972).

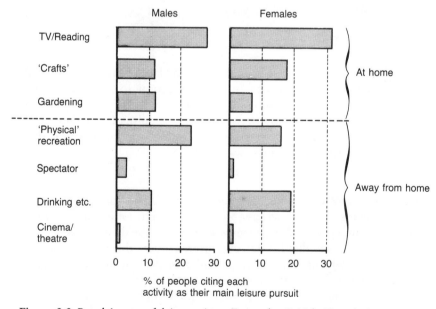

Figure 2.3 People's use of leisure time. From the British Travel Association (1967).

recreation. The figure shows that these parameters have a positive corre-
lation with the amount of time/money individuals spend on leisure pursuits. Figure 2.3 shows the type of leisure pursuits that people followed
in 1966 (British Travel Association, 1967). From this early work, many
of the basic features of leisure activity which are now readily accepted,
began to emerge: the seasonality of the leisure industry; the different
activities followed by different socio-economic and domestic groups; the
dominance of car users; and the use made of the countryside within
the wide leisure spectrum.

Clawson and Knetsch (1966) attempted to draw some dividing lines
between formal leisure activities and what is now viewed as countryside
recreation. They developed the concept of 'user-oriented' recreation and
'resource-based' recreation – a model that was applied to outdoor recreation. The 'resource-based outdoor' recreation equates fairly closely
with the modern concepts of countryside recreation, and still forms a
good starting point for a definition; some recreational activity is dependent upon scarce resources, and indeed the activity is based largely upon
the attraction of the land or the resource itself, in many cases regardless
of the facilities on it.

Early, general studies of leisure and recreation led, in the 1970s, to a
closer assessment of elements within the overall picture. The most relevant area of study for our purposes was countryside recreation. The
importance of countryside recreation was mirrored by corresponding
legislation (Bromley, 1990). The main thrust of this legislation was to
create powers (primarily for local authorities in Britain) to develop
resources to accommodate the demand for countryside recreation –
country parks, picnic sites and recreational routes, for example. The
relevant Acts of Parliament (Department of the Environment, 1967,
1968) also created the Countryside Commission for Scotland and for
England and Wales. Both of these organizations had a joint remit to
provide for countryside recreation and natural beauty and amenity. The
Countryside Commissions implement their policies by advising government ministers, grant-aiding private and public sector providers and
undertaking research (giving advice to the public).

The 1970s, therefore, witnessed a growing interest in countryside
recreation, (Figure 2.5) which was reflected in legislation and in the
increasing demand for access to the countryside. Coppock and Duffield
(1975) produced a detailed analysis of recreation in the countryside
which drew the distinction between active countryside recreation and
passive countryside recreation. This distinction is helpful in that it allows
managers to determine what facilities might be provided on-site. However, it is clear that no hard and fast definitions can be made that allow

Figure 2.4 The National Trust has for many years been one of Britain's most important providers of recreational opportunities.

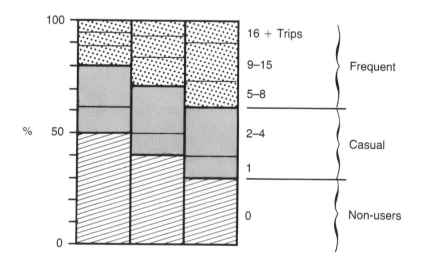

Figure 2.5 Proportion of people making countryside trips. From Countryside Commission (1985) *Household Recreation Survey.*

us to determine whether any particular site provides for active or passive countryside recreation.

In practice, most sites will provide both. As Coppock and Duffield suggest 'In principle, establishing what resources are actually used for outdoor recreation should be a simple matter of survey, but . . . this is not so in practice . . . Informal passive recreation shows more character-istics to a marked degree' (Coppock and Duffield, 1975, p 96).

Many studies have been undertaken in an effort to fully understand the nature and causes of demand for countryside recreation (Duffield and Owen, 1970; Countryside Commission, 1985; Centre for Leisure Research, 1986). Any over-simplification of the large amount of data would be misleading; some trends are, however, worthy of note. Figures 2.6 and 2.7 show a series of parameters for people visiting the country-side and the activities that they pursue. As a summary of these trends, the Countryside Policy Review Panel (1987) state 'that current trends show little lessening of demand . . . More important are changes in the way the countryside is used for recreation. Greater emphasis on active pursuits is now evident . . . Other comparatively new activities have been estab-lished in a rural setting, such as theme or safari parks, and organised sports'. However, of equal importance is the fact that a large majority of people still derive the greatest pleasure from the simple activity of walking in or looking at the countryside.

These statistics present the manager with his or her greatest challenge; providing a resource that attracts and interests people sufficiently (in many cases, sufficiently to ask the public to pay for the experience) but does not destroy or detract from the very resource that the public have come to see. The point at which a countryside recreation site becomes a recreation site which happens to be based in a rural setting is a very grey one; working definitions will change. For some, countryside recreation means walking in the Scottish Highlands away from most other people. To others it means an intensively managed site with a visitor centre, cafe, play facilities and a large car park. The question is one of degree, rather than kind, but most managers will need to make some very basic decisions about the type of resource they will manage.

In summary, therefore, the latter part of the 20th century has witnessed a large increase in demand for leisure opportunities. Furthermore, the more specific demand for countryside recreation has also increased. This specific demand has been mirrored by a legislative framework and by a continuing effort to understand the causes and implications of the demand for countryside recreation. What is clear is that the demand looks set to continue and that the nature of the demand will change as new experiences are sought. The manager must seek to meet at least

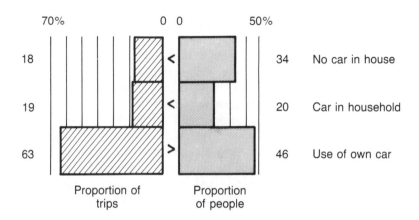

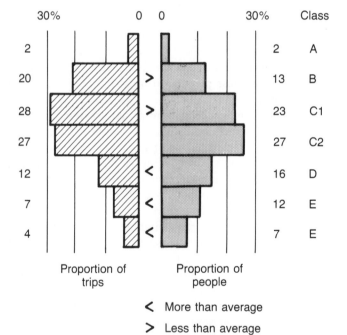

Figure 2.6 (a) Trips to the countryside by car ownership. (b) Trips to the countryside by social class. From Countryside Commission (1985) *Household Recreation Survey.*

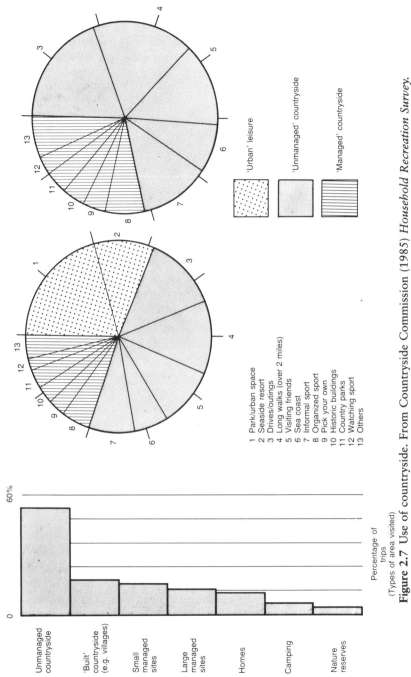

Figure 2.7 Use of countryside. From Countryside Commission (1985) *Household Recreation Survey*.

1 Park/urban space
2 Seaside resort
3 Drives/outings
4 Long walks (over 2 miles)
5 Visiting friends
6 Sea coast
7 Informal sport
8 Organized sport
9 Pick your own
10 Historic buildings
11 Country parks
12 Watching sport
13 Others

'Urban' leisure

'Unmanaged' countryside

'Managed' countryside

60%

0

Percentage of
trips
(Types of area visited)

Unmanaged
countryside

'Built'
countryside
(e.g. villages)

Small
managed
sites

Large
managed
sites

Homes

Camping

Nature
reserves

some of this demand, without relinquishing his or her obligations to protect and enhance the basic integrity of the countryside which attracts so many people.

2.3 COUNTRYSIDE RECREATION IN BRITAIN

The existing range of countryside recreation sites in Britain is as great as anywhere in Europe, possibly the world. Britain offers the opportunity of the solitary beauty of the Cairngorms or the Welsh Marches and intensively managed, but none the less stimulating environment of the urban fringe, in the Lee Valley Regional Park, for example (Turner, 1988). For the manager, either private or public, there needs to be a good deal of analysis and decision making to determine where on this continuum of types of facility his or her particular site will be situated. In order to have a national framework in which to place a particular site, we need first to look at the overall picture of provision for countryside recreation in Britain.

Any assessment of provision will include a wide range of groups and individuals. These will range from private sector operators (country estates, specialist parks or open farms, for example) voluntary organizations (such as the National Trust, the Royal Society for the Protection of Birds or local county conservation trusts) and the public sector (County Councils, District Councils or, in Scotland, Regional Councils). The dividing lines between these types of organizations are becoming increasingly blurred – if they were ever clear in the first place. Furthermore, the actual number of individual sites is impossible to gauge, so a checklist cannot be considered. The following analysis is, therefore, based upon types of provision rather than a site-by-site assessments.

2.3.1 Wilderness areas

The wilderness in Britain is restricted to very small areas of land, left as vestiges of virgin habitats such as the remnant of the Caledonian Forests or the Humber Levels. For the purposes of this discussion, therefore, wilderness in Britain can be used to define the remote relatively inaccessible areas that lie outside the realms of intensive management. Areas thus defined would include many of the Scottish upland areas, parts of the English and Welsh National Parks and some lowland or wetland areas such as the Flow County in Caithness or the Mosses and Meres of western England. For countryside recreation managers, these areas represent delicate and intricate places (and ownerships are often many and varied, the habitats and landscapes are complex and their boundaries are vague or nebulous). As Table 2.1 indicates, however, these areas are attractive for countryside recreation. Where land ownership is relatively simple because it lies within a single holding, management is made easier. This is the case, for example, in private estate lands that are managed, at least in parts, for countryside recreation. Similarly, several voluntary or charitable organizations own and manage large tracts of open wilderness, again partly for recreational purposes (the National Trust, for example, own many large sites throughout Britain which cater for countryside recreation).

Countryside sites in Britain's wilderness areas tend to be managed on a low-key basis not only because of the relative inaccessibility of the areas but also because of the delicate nature of the environments. Where this pattern is not followed, conflicts of opinion often occur (Nature Conservancy Council, 1987, gives an assessment of the impacts of intensive provision for skiing in the Cairngorms and Glen Shee).

2.3.2 Accessible countryside

Most, if not all, of Britain's countryside is accessible. Certain areas are, however, more accessible because of their proximity to urban centres, the quality of the transport network or because of the provision made for public access. Thus, many areas, particularly in lowland Britain, are under intensive pressure from people seeking countryside recreation. The countryside manager can provide for this in a variety of ways: country parks; open farms; estate land; picnic sites; nature trails and water-based sites are just a few. The management of each of these facilities will have features and methods common to all the others. The nature of these sites means that, in general, they tend to be smaller than the more remote areas. This is for various reasons: the obvious constraints on space; the economic pressure on land which tends to restrict the size to which any resource can grow; and the types of facility provided. The Countryside Commission of England and the Countryside Councils of Wales and Scotland have seen this accessible countryside as being of equal importance as the remoter areas. Hence, their concern for the provision of country parks, urban fringe projects and the upgrading (in England and Wales) of the public-right-of-way network.

2.3.3 Local countryside

More recent provision of countryside recreation sites has tended to focus upon the neighbourhood level. Innovative work at West Midlands

County Council (1984) and Tyne and Wear County Council (Nature Conservancy Council, 1988) led to a wide acceptance that the countryside does not stop at the edge of the urban area neither does the demand for countryside recreation. Within local areas, therefore, pocket parks, urban trails, and schools nature areas are all manifestations of this demand for localized countryside recreation. Ownership and management of these sites tends to be markedly different from that of, say, an open farm or private estate land. Urban sites tend to be owned and managed by the local community, either through the Local Authority or through trusts such as Groundwork Trust or residents associations. For the manager, however, they represent an extreme on the continuum of countryside recreation sites.

2.4 COUNTRYSIDE RECREATION: THE PROVIDERS

The picture of a variety of types of countryside recreation sites is further complicated by the numbers of different providers of countryside recreation sites. Rogers *et al.* (1985), for example, lists over 50 groups and organizations that provide different types of countryside recreation. These include Local Authorities (at County, District and Regional level), the National Trust, the Royal Society for the Protection of Birds, the Forestry Commission, private estates and individuals, Water Authorities and many more. The list is by no means comprehensive, because within the generic term 'private estates' many hundreds of countryside recreation sites are represented; from a large working estate such as Chatsworth in Derbyshire or Blenheim Palace in Oxfordshire, which provide an element of countryside recreation, to small, privately managed open farms or rural centres.

For the public, therefore, there is a dazzling array of types of provision and potential providers. It is small wonder that the lay person becomes confused by the terms associated with the countryside and the differences between them: nature reserve, area of outstanding natural beauty, farm trail, forest park and so on.

For the manager, this multifaceted picture represents the physical and economic environment within which he or she must work. Physical, in the sense that managers of the countryside must not forget that the resource for which they are responsible is part of a larger and wider ecosystem. Economic, in the sense that all managers, to a greater or lesser extent, want to attract people to visit their site as opposed to one of the many alternatives. That decision, made by the public, is at least partly an economic decision.

Figure 2.8 The coast and the seaside remain a popular destination for outdoor recreation.

Management of the countryside for recreation is not entirely dependent upon ownership. For Local Authorities and voluntary charitable trusts ownership and management are usually undertaken by the same organization, although, compulsory competitive tendering of Local Authority Services has begun to change this situation (see section 4.4 for further discussion). For many private concerns, however, management is a separate function from ownership. In all cases, however, ownership will inevitably have a major impact upon management objectives and techniques. Land ownership patterns in the countryside are, however, much slower to change than those in urban areas. As Rogers *et al.* (1985) suggest 'Traditional land ownership is in decline, and institutional land ownership is on the increase, but less than 2 per cent of farmland changes hands every year, so ownership patterns will be slow to change'.

2.5 SITE-BASED PROVISION

It is evident that managers of countryside recreation sites work in a very dynamic socio-economic and physical environment whilst some elements (such as ownership) only change slowly. For the individual site manager, therefore, there are a number of key decisions that need to be made before the day-to-day management of the site begins.

Many of these key issues are discussed in the next chapter, where the process of management planning is analysed. Within the broader context here, there are still some central issues which need to be resolved.

2.5.1 Ownership

The ownership of the site will, to a large extent, determine not only the type of recreational site provided, but also the method of management. A Local Authority, for example, can have only limited levels of profit from direct trading operations, whilst this clearly does not apply to a private or public liability company. Equally, a Local Authority has certain statutory obligations which it must perform, whereas trusts or private organizations do not have these statutory obligations but are clearly bound by other legal requirements. The manager of a countryside recreation site must, therefore, establish the ownership structure of the land for which he or she is responsible. This will influence many of the parameters within which the manager operates.

2.5.2 Type of provision

A broad understanding of the type of provision to be made is a necessary prerequisite of management. Whilst such an understanding must never pre-empt or replace a detailed management planning process, it is clearly necessary to provide a broad framework. Is the site to be profit led, for example, or a resource that is free at source (at least to start with)? Is it to provide intensive recreational experience, or is the value of the landscape paramount. These policy decisions will arise from several interacting influences: ownership, area of land, type of landscape/topography, location, natural history interests. Whilst a detailed survey of all of these issues is needed as part of the planning and management process, an assessment of overall policy is needed to initiate the management process.

2.5.3 Wider implications

All countryside recreation sites fit within a regional and national perspective which has many facets. Many areas are covered by landscape policies or nature conservation strategies, for example. These may be prepared by local planning authorities or national agencies such as the Countryside Commission or Countryside Councils. Similarly, most areas will be covered by recreation plans or strategies, prepared again by the Local Authorities or the Sports Council. These elements of the wider physical, economic and recreational environment may bring constraints (in the shape of certain restrictions imposed on development or through a desire by the manager to fit within these frameworks) or opportunities (through possible grant aid or support for projects, for example).

In developing a starting point for managing a countryside recreation site, the manager must therefore, initially map out some of the underlying principles that will guide the management of the site. Often, these underlying principles may be left unsaid or unrecorded, but in order for the manager to understand fully his or her responsibilities they must be explored.

The process of exploring the principles is comparable with developing a brief for a design process (Greenstreet, 1980). Having prepared this brief, the manager can then proceed with the evaluation of the site and subsequently, the management planning for the site. This is the subject of the next chapter.

Management planning | 3

3.1 INTRODUCTION

The management process begins with a thorough assessment, not only of the resource or the land to be managed, but also of the proposals for the land, the expectations of the management, how their expectations will be measured and projections for the future development of the site. The underlying principles of management, therefore, form no more than a start to a detailed process.

The form that management planning takes may vary from one organization to another, but despite these individual characteristics there are a number of key steps that need to be taken which are common to all management planning. Preparing a management plan is central to the success of any venture, and the success of a countryside recreation site is no different. The main variation between sites will be how success is defined, but careful planning is integral to all site management. This chapter analyses the process of preparing the management plan and discusses the various stages that are necessary. The link that the management plan has with other strategies is also explored; business plans, corporate strategies and marketing policies may all assume greater importance at some sites than at others.

Finally the chapter examines some of the processes involved with managing the site once a plan has been developed.

It will soon become evident that the process of management planning is not a static or one-off activity; it is continuous. So too is the process of management *per se*. It is not possible to establish a framework that can be left to run on its own. The manager must, therefore, be prepared not only to plan, but also to control the process once it is in operation.

3.2 MANAGEMENT PLANS

Almost every organization that is responsible for managing land used for countryside recreation, or for advising those who manage such land, has its own method for preparing management plans. The Countryside Commission, English Nature, the National Trust, English Heritage and county or wildlife conservation trusts, therefore, all have their own approaches to the subject. These methods have been analysed elsewhere (Wood and Warren, 1978; Nature Conservancy Council, 1983; Leay Rowe and Young, 1986, for example) and the model chosen here is the most straightforward. None the less, it serves to identify the key elements in the preparation of the managements plan. Figure 3.1 gives a diagrammatic representation of the process.

The key stages are: the assessment of the aim of managing the site; a survey of the site and its immediate physical, cultural and economic environment; an analysis of the survey results; the setting of management objectives; the development of management prescriptions; initiating the implementation of the plan; and monitoring the success of the process.

Before each of these key stages is dealt with in more detail, it is worth stressing that the manager is involved with all stages of management planning, from policy formulation, through implementation to monitoring and review. Indeed, not only is the job satisfaction of the manager increased if this rule is followed, but the efficiency of plan implementation is greatly increased. The management plan is, therefore, all embracing, but first and foremost a working document. As Leay, Rowe and Young, point out 'The plan is a vehicle for recording systematically the characteristics of a site, acknowledging explicitly its most valuable aspect and specifying objectives for the site's management which will be achieved through the proposals and work programmes which are outlined in the plan' (Leay, Rowe and Young, 1986).

3.2.1 Aims

The aims of the management plan will reflect broad policies that will underpin the planning and management processes. These may develop from corporate aims; where the recreation site is one of a number owned by the same organization. Alternatively, they may be the policies of a single group for a single site. Whatever the case, the underlying principles need to be recorded because they will form the basis of all subsequent decision making. Thus, for example, if profit maximization is the main concern, this would be an aim. Similarly, if the provision of informal

Aims

A broad statement of the policies which will underlie management of the land – indicating the intended balance to be achieved between the various land uses and interests

Survey

A comprehensive record of what is present on the land and how it is managed, forming a baseline for the analysis and statement of objectives. Influences and constraints external to the land are included

Analysis

An examination of the options for management of the land and the interrelationship between existing and potential land uses. Potential problems and conflicts are identified and the various interests are weighed against one another. From the decisions reached, objectives are formulated.

Management objectives

Specific statements on how the AIMS are to be pursued in the longer term – at a general level; in the shorter term – within each area of landuse and interest.

Management prescription

An overview of the work required and the resources needed to achieve the MANAGEMENT OBJECTIVES.

Implementation

Details of the integrated action programme drawn up from the overall requirement of work to be done, and by which the MANAGEMENT OBJECTIVES will be achieved. Yearly programmes are developed at this stage.

Monitoring and review

A record and assessment of management achievements together with proposals for periodic review.

Figure 3.1 Typical headings in a management plan.

OBJECTIVES:	Policies; priorities; broad vision for site.
SITE HISTORY:	Ownership; policy status; management history.
RECREATION:	Use; potential; existing facilities.
FUTURE USE:	Markets available; local trends; competition; seasonal trends; external consideration.
MANAGEMENT:	Implementation; land management; management structure; resources required.
REVIEW:	Review; monitoring; measures of success.

Figure 3.2 A summary of the production of a management plan. From Leay, Rowe and Young (1986).

countryside recreation for disadvantaged groups is of importance, this too would be an aim.

It is evident that any single site will have a number of aims, so it is important not only to balance these against each other (which the management plan itself will endeavour to do) but also to prioritize these aims. This will allow the manager and anyone who subsequently may take over management of the site, to identify the most important aim, and those of lesser importance, but which none the less require consideration.

For many managers, the aim may already be established: Local Authorities, for example, will have political and management aims as part of their wider operation, as too will most private and voluntary sector organizations. There too, it is important that these principles are recorded as aims within the management plan.

After reading the aims it should be possible to establish very clearly what the management of the site seeks to achieve, so they should be concise, but above all clear.

3.2.2 Survey

The single most important basis for sound decision making is good information. 'Good' includes many parameters, such as relevant, clear, descriptive, qualitative and quantitative.

By and large, the survey and the detail in which certain areas are covered, will depend upon the aims of the countryside site. A country park, for example, which seeks to provide informal recreation for a local centre of population will not require a survey that dwells too long on alternative sites of outstanding natural history importance; clearly it is of relevance, but priorities may lie elsewhere.

As a guide, the survey should cover two broad areas of study: site survey and overall context.

3.2.3 The site survey

The site survey should cover all of the important features of the site; Leay, Rowe and Young (1986) suggest 13 such categories, namely:

1. Area, occupancy, legal background and leases;
2. Summary of land use, existing and historical;
3. Buildings;
4. Topography;
5. Aspect, climate, local weather;
6. Geology and soils;
7. Landscape character, diversity, key elements or components;
8. Habitat for wildlife, special species;
9. Historical and archaeological features;
10. Cultural associations, literary, artistic or traditional;
11. Public rights of way (permissive, definitive, informal), recreational use of area;
12. Legal constraints, tenants, easements or covenants;
13. Income generated, areas of immediate expenditure.

The importance attached to each of these categories will reflect the aims and obviously, the basic nature of the site. Indeed it is not unlikely that the aims may need to be modified in the light of the survey. Hence, it is useful to consider the setting of aims and the survey as two parts of the same, initial stage of preparing a management plan.

The overall context aspect of the survey ensures that the site does not sit in isolation from the surrounding environment. This is important for ecological and landscape reasons, because the overall integrity of the countryside must be protected. It is also important for other reasons. If the facility is to be self-financing, for example, it is important to fully understand the alternative sites in the area or region that might attract visitors. Similarly, any recreation resource that seeks to attract relatively large numbers of visitors will need to include, as part of its survey and assessment, relevant external demographic, transport and socio-economic details.

The broader survey should, therefore, include details of the regional and local setting, of population, the local planning framework, statutory designations, trends, pressures and alternative sites, all of which have an impact on the development of a countryside recreation site.

Figure 3.3 The location of the car-park is one of the simplest, yet most important decisions to be made by the manager.

3.2.4 Analysis

The analysis of the survey results involves assessing the implication of existing and possible land uses in the light of the aims of the management. It is inevitable that proposals will be in conflict, for example, a possible route for a footpath may well cross a valuable natural history site. Similarly, the most accessible point of a site may be the most visible, which means that proposals for car parking will have to be carefully considered. These potential conflicts need to be identified and resolved in the analysis stage of the plan preparation.

In this respect, the analysis marks the point of the planning process during which most of the management decisions are made. For this reason, it is also evident that the managers personal preferences may influence the decisions. It is, therefore, imperative that these personal preferences are identified, so that subsequent confusion does not arise.

The analysis may be undertaken on a land use basis, with issues such as recreation, forestry, natural history and archaeology, for example, being studied separately before being brought together. For a large site, this is appropriate, as within each of the separate categories, hierarchies will need to be developed. For small sites, however, it is appropriate that the site be reviewed as a whole.

3.2.5 Objectives

Having brought together the broad aims of the manager and the physical opportunities and constraints that operate within and around the site, the manager must set tight objectives to guide the management process.

Setting objectives forms the point at which the manager can begin to control events. The objectives determine what courses of action are followed, how they are to be undertaken, how results are to be measured and how the management process is to be monitored. Hence, it is important that the objectives are specific and clear, and that they follow logically on from the original aims.

The aims can be considered as general statements of intent but the objectives translate these general intentions into measurable and precise targets. Thus, the general 'aim' of 'increasing the enjoyment of existing and repeat visitors' could translate into the specific objectives of:

- staging a series of 12 guided walks over the summer period;
- increasing the number of interpretive display panels on the site;
- ensure that all paths are waymarked and have a passable surface for 12 months of the year.

These objectives can be measured, priced and given a timetable for implementation. Thus, they provide a clear starting point for the decision making process.

The objectives and the targets that are set by them, become more critical when the overall viability of the site is dependent upon meeting financial objectives. In this context objectives might be considered in terms of increasing visitor spend per visit by 20% or increasing visitor numbers by 15%. This may be further detailed by identifying target groups, such as school parties, families, off-peak visitors and so on. Obviously, these objectives could equally be used for public sector facilities, but might include references to disadvantaged groups, disabled visitors or other groups; this would, however, depend upon the socio-political aims of the organization.

Objectives will probably reflect both short-term and long-term commitments. For this reason, and also because it is very easy for a plan to become outdated, objectives (and indeed the overall plan) should be given a timescale. Usually, this is 3 or 5 years. The advantage of having short- and long-term objectives is that whilst short-term objectives can be dealt with immediately, long-term objectives can form the basis of policy and strategy discussions. Thus, once the short-term objectives have been met, the longer term objectives can be brought forward at plan review and reframed as short-term objectives. This means that the planning process is continuous, rather than a series of 'stops' and 'starts'.

3.2.6 Management prescriptions

The role of the manager is to deal with all elements of the continuum from policy development to scheme implementation and monitoring. Thus, the manager has to ensure that the objectives are actually implemented on the ground. The management prescriptions represent the first stage in the implementation process. The prescription will inevitably be phased over the period of time that the plan covers – usually 3 or 5 years. Furthermore, the detail that the prescription includes will vary; work for immediate implementation will require a high degree of detail, whilst work that will only be implemented in the medium-term future may well be in sketch or draft detail.

However, the prescriptions whether or not they are detailed, must in themselves meet a number of objectives.

- They must allow a detailed work programme to be developed on an annual basis, and allow schemes and projects to be rolled forward as necessary.
- They must identify the necessary labour resources and what type of labour will be used: voluntary, own staff, contract labour and so on.
- The requirement for any materials that need to be specifically identified and whether they should be purchased as part of the overall maintenance requirement or hired or provided through contractors.
- The prescriptions should also enable the manager to identify financial resources that are required. These may be in the form of detailed quotations for the individual element of work, or the estimates for work not yet fully identified.

The prescription should, therefore, give an overview of the process necessary to meet the management objectives. This closely fits into the next stage of the plan process, namely implementation.

3.2.7 Implementation

In much the same way that management objectives give detail and a degree of control over the aims of the management plan, so the process of implementation gives detail and control to the prescription.

Implementation, the control of the physical tasks necessary to undertake the prescription, is usually the responsibility of one person within an organization. Whether this person is helped by other staff depends upon the relative size of the operation. However, an overall coordinator of projects does allow all the necessary financial, personnel and contractual information to be channelled through one person. In very small organizations, this single channel may well be the overall site manager, but often, the scheme implementation falls to a separate individual.

The format of the work programme will depend upon the complexities of the site. For a very small site, an annotated plan may suffice (Figure 3.4, for example). However, more usually, a greater degree of detail is required, fully prepared and scheduled by a qualified landscape consultant. Where work is to be undertaken by contract labour this is critical. Where volunteers are involved, however, it is less important, not least because volunteers cannot usually read bills of quantities. This identifies why a broad overview, by way of the prescriptions, should precede the implementation stage.

3.2.8 Monitoring

The process of monitoring is continuous and will fall into several stages. However, at each stage the monitoring process will have similar characteristics.

First, in order to monitor effectively, it is necessary to have clear targets against which performance can be reviewed. Thus, the objectives must be clear and concise. When the objectives are being set, therefore, it is necessary to have half-a-mind on how they will be monitored. For example, the objective of increasing visitor numbers by 15% will require, *inter alia*, a system for counting visitor numbers. The objective of raising visitor enjoyment will require a more subjective and detailed information gathering process. Finally, the objective of increasing the number of resident great crested grebes will unquestionably require further resources!

Secondly, the process of monitoring will also require a high level of usable information. What information is collected will depend upon the objectives and the methods of monitoring, but clearly the information should relate directly to the objectives; thus, financial, socio-economic,

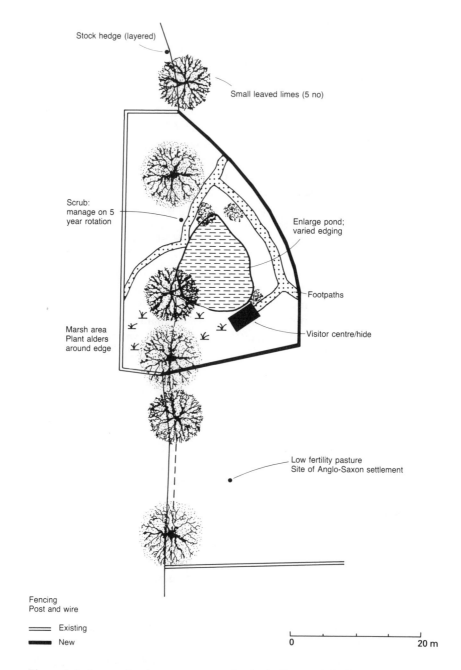

Stock hedge (layered)

Small leaved limes (5 no)

Scrub:
manage on 5
year rotation

Enlarge pond;
varied edging

Footpaths

Marsh area
Plant alders
around edge

Visitor centre/hide

Low fertility pasture
Site of Anglo-Saxon settlement

Fencing
Post and wire

Existing

New

0   20 m

Figure 3.4 A very simple management plan including prescriptions.

subjective and biological information may all be required by the manager during the monitoring process.

Finally, the monitoring process is not complete if action is not taken to overcome any deviations between expected and actual outcomes. There can be any one of many reasons why there is a deviation, but identifying the causes and (if possible and necessary) doing something about them, is the role of the manager.

The type of information and the regularity with which it is reviewed will both vary. Financial cash flows may have to be monitored monthly (or perhaps more frequently during peak times) whereas the environmental impact of a new footpath may best be monitored bi-annually or annually.

3.2.9 Survey work

The concept of monitoring logically raises the need for surveys. The numerous techniques available and necessary for the manager are related to the many facets of the site that will require survey. Clearly many of these techniques will match those used in the original site survey; habitat diversity or through-puts of visitor numbers need to be recorded with comparable methods in order to ensure that the results are themselves comparable.

The Nature Conservancy Council provided guidelines for habitat survey using their Phase 1 and Phase 2 survey techniques. Over a period of time, the survey methodology will allow qualitative and quantitative changes to be measured.

The Countryside Commission offer guidelines for surveys of landscape and visitors to countryside recreation sites (Countryside Commission, 1988, 1985c). Similarly, the Tourism and Recreation Research Unit have produced guidelines for visitor surveys on countryside recreation sites (Tourism and Recreation Research Unit, 1983).

The most important issue when undertaking a survey is to understand clearly the objectives of the study; what is actually being measured and why. If the survey simply seeks to collect a large amount of data for no particular reason, a very costly and possibly misleading set of data will be the only result.

3.2.10 Review

After the plan has run its prescribed course, it will be necessary to review the whole plan. Plan review must be put into motion before the original management plan expires so that continuity is maintained.

The review process may also be brought forward by a major change in the circumstances of the countryside site; a change of ownership, major short falls in through flow of cash or in local government, a change of political backing!

The review must be a thorough assessment of the whole plan and the means by which it is implemented. Thus, the aims of the manager must be reassessed and if necessary the survey work must also be undertaken again. Following on from this, the objectives, prescriptions and methods of implementation and monitoring must also be reviewed.

3.2.11 Summary

Producing a management plan is simply a matter of following a sequence of activities that lead logically from the formulation of ideas to the implementation of schemes and the monitoring of progress. The plan is both a means of controlling future events, by outlining work programmes and a means of managing the process of change, by providing a framework within which change can operate. The plan also gives a yardstick against which the progress on-site can be measured.

It is, therefore, vital that the management plan is a working document and does not become a dusty document kept on an inaccessible shelf or in a drawer. To this end, the manager must decide the optimum format for the management plan for his or her particular site.

3.3 BUSINESS PLANS

The management plan equips the manager with a means of establishing aims, objectives and methods for achieving these objectives. The business plan provides the same balance of forecasts and control over the financial and other affairs of the countryside business. One looks at a site, the other at the business – both need each other.

Many organizations develop the business plan as a separate entity to the management plan. This will depend upon the scale and amount of money involved in managing a site. Some organizations such as the National Trust, include the business plan as part of the management plan (Leay, Rowe and Young, 1986). Whilst others, such as Groundwork Trusts, prepare separate business plans for their work (Wakefield Groundwork Trust, 1989).

The purpose of a business plan is not simply to record levels of income and expenditure; that is done through the accounts system. A business plan sets financial targets for the management of the countryside site,

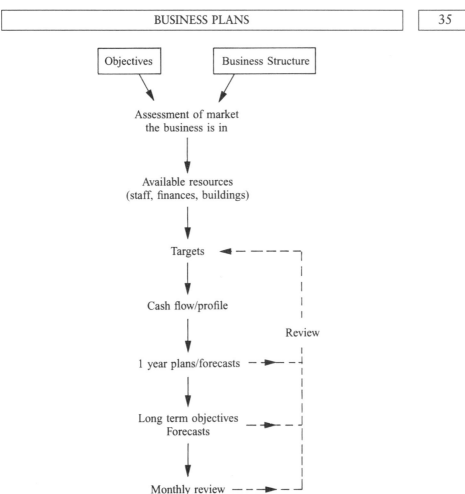

Figure 3.5 Business plan production: key stages.

and analyses the financial requirements of the organizations in more detail than the management plan. It also looks at the resources needed to accomplish tasks, including volunteers, office support and so on.

The business plan should cover a number of key topics outlined below.

3.3.1 Objectives

In order for the business plan to link into the overall management plan, the business plan should also set out the management plan objectives. The financial aims should be identified as well. One such broad aim might be 'to secure a sound financial structure and strong operating base for the organization'. This will be translated into objectives such as: 'increase average visitor spending to £2.00 per head' or 'increase visitor numbers by 5% per annum in the plan period'.

Whatever the objectives, clearly they should be common to the management plan and the business plan, although in the latter it is possible to explore financial objectives in more detail.

3.3.2 Strategy

The business plan will usually be a relatively technical document, dealing with visitor numbers, income, expenditure, profits and loss. By way of an introduction to this information and as an overview, it is important to discuss the strategy that will be adopted to meet objectives. If, for example, the organization is seeking to target a particular section of the community, this should be explored within the strategy. Similarly, charging and fee generating policies should also be explained.

Unless this information is given within the business plan, the financial and other projections will stand in isolation from any fixed point of reference and, for this reason, will at best be meaningless and at worst misleading. Within the public sector, for example, levels of grant aid forecasted within the business plan need to be substantiated within the strategy. For the private or voluntary sector, increases in membership or increases in visitor numbers have to be based on an understanding and analysis of the existing situation.

3.3.3 Resources and assets

The business plan should also contain an analysis, however brief, of the resources that the site has which, within a strictly financial analysis, may be overlooked. It is important to remember that the environment can never be reduced to simply financial terms.

These additional resources may include: the special features of the sites; additional expertise available to the site management through existing staff, the organization within which the site operates or other contacts; and material that the manager or site may have inherited. (It is rare that a countryside recreation site materializes out of a formerly derelict and unused facility – more often a site offers some existing potential and hence resources.)

3.3.4 Financial analysis

The heart of the business plan lives within the financial analysis of income and expenditure (or profits and loss) for the plan period. Clearly, it is necessary to link the business plan and management plan together to the same timescale.

The aim of the financial analysis is to give a clear guide to not only prediction about future performance but also to establish, in the case of private sector operation, the levels at which the countryside site ceases to be financially viable.

Table 3.1 shows a financial assessment of an upland estate, with projected income and expenditure levels over a 5 year period. In this

Table 3.1 Upland estate management costs (National Trust managed)

Item	Year 1	2	3	4	5
Income					
Farm rents	7000	7000	7000	7000	7000
Other rents and licences (riding permits)	70	70	70	70	70
House/cottage – rents (10 cottages)	10 850	10 850	10 850	10 850	10 850
Woods – timber sales (and grants FGS/BWS)	1000	–	–	–	–
Visitors (cairns)	200	200	200	200	200
Government grants	20 000	10 000			
Finance – investment income	–	–		–	
Countryside Commission grant:					
25% of wages	4000	4000	4000	?	?
Shop	500	700	700	700	700
Recruiting credits					
Total income	43 620	32 820	Years 3–5 roll forward		
Expenditure					
Farm repairs	1500	1500	1500	1500	1500
House/cottage repairs, services and supplies	8500	8500	8500	8500	8500
Woods – supplies	500	2500	2500	2500	2500
Estate general – wages: 2 wardens 1 seasonal	16 000	16 000	16 000	16 000	16 000
Estate general – supplies, vehicles, etc.	5000	5000	5000	5000	5000
Government costs	20 000	10 000			
General/miscellaneous	4000	4000			
Subtotal	55 500	47 500	Not predictable		
Management charge at 20%	11 100	9500			
Insurance	1000	1000	1000	1000	1000
Total expenditure	67 600	58 000	Years 3–5 roll forward		
Net total (recurring)	–23 980	–25 180			

Source: Countryside Commission (1986) *Management Plan: Preparation and Development*

case, the figures relate to a national organization, the National Trust, and the recurring loss will be supported by national sources of finance, most usually from money raised by membership and donations. This introduces a further important factor about both the business plan and the management plan; their place within wider, corporate strategies.

Where, however, a site must stand in isolation and must also be financially viable, no such loss can be continued indefinitely. Table 3.2 identifies a basic spreadsheet with information about an operation in this position. Within such an analysis, there are several areas of uncertainty, for example, visitor numbers, spending levels, interest rates and the cost of salaries and wages over the plan period. However, the plan must begin to identify these individual areas of income and expenditure. Similarly, the uncertainty emphasizes the need to monitor closely predicted levels against actual levels.

The level at which the manager becomes involved in the detailed analysis of interest rates, salaries negotiations and so on depends very much upon the size of the organization. In a small operation, the manager may be expected to hold this level of information. In most situations, however, expert financial advice will be available and, therefore, the manager must be concerned with the broader implication of the business plan and its relationship to the management plan. For most managers this management plan will provide additional detail to the overall plan, not vice versa. In short, money allows the manager to meet his or her environmental or recreational objectives.

In order to complete the assessment of countryside site business plans, Table 3.3 gives an example of a financial analysis of a public sector operation. It is evident that whilst the sources of income are vastly different (grant aid and core funding as opposed to visitor income) the information is very similar. Indeed, the distinction between private and public sector operation is becoming increasingly blurred; many public sector countryside sites being expected to return some money to offset the cost of the site to the Local Authority's central budgets. Similarly, many private countryside sites also attract central and local government grants for their recreational and conservation work.

3.3.5 Monitoring

Finally the business plan should also carry some reference to how the plan will be monitored. Income for the site, number of visitors and visitor expenditure will all need to be recorded, as too will levels of expenditure by the manager.

Monitoring income will depend upon the method of visitor control

Table 3.2 Basic information required for business plan for single site operation

Country park: Income and expenditure

| Year | Predicted attendance | Income per head | Gross income (£) | Expenditure analysis | | Other at 16.5p per head | Gross expenditure | P/L excl. interest on borrowing |
				Salaries and wages	Maintenance and repairs			
1	40 000	70p	28 000	35 000	6000	6600	47 600	-19 600
2	55 000	£1	55 000	35 000	8000	9075	52 075	+ 2 925
3	75 000	£1	75 000	40 000	10 000	12 375	62 375	+12 625
4	75 000	£1	75 000	40 000	10 000	12 375	62 375	+12 625
5	100 000	£1	100 000	45 000	10 000	16 500	71 500	+28 500
6	100 000	£1	100 000	45 000	10 000	16 500	71 500	+28 500
7	100 000	£1	100 000	45 000	10 000	16 500	71 500	+28 500

Country park: Bank borrowing and interests

Year	Borrowing at start of year	Predicted visitor numbers	Gross income	Expenditure	Interest on borrowing at start of year	Net profit (+) loss (−)
0						
1	35 000	40 000	28 000	47 600	5250	-24 850
2	59 850	55 000	55 000	52 075	6052	− 6052
3	65 902	75 000	75 000	62 375	9885	+ 2740
4	63 162	75 000	75 000	62 375	9474	+ 3151
5	60 011	100 000	100 000	71 500	9001	+19 499
6	40 512	100 000	100 000	71 500	6076	+22 424
7	32 852	100 000	100 000	71 500	4928	+23 572

Table 3.3 Business plan details from a small charitable trust

	1992/3	1993/4	1994/5	1995/6	1996/7
Income					
Government grants	80 000	65 000	45 000	37 221	35 000
LA's	50 000	52 500	55 125	57 881	60 775
Private sector	6000	–	–	–	–
Trust	15 158	24 722	45 538	53 000	60 000
C/over (approx.)	50 000	45 000	45 000	45 000	45 000
UK 2000	10 000	15 000	15 000	15 000	15 000
Countryside Commission	15 000	15 000	15 000	15 000	15 000
Project grants	10 000	10 000	10 000	10 000	10 000
Thematics/events	18 000	8000	8000	8000	8000
	254 158	235 222	238 663	241 102	248 775
Expenditure					
Salaries	139 503	146 478	153 801	161 491	169 565
Recruit/train	3000	3000	2000	2000	2500
Travel	4000	5000	5000	5000	5500
Office	16 000	17 000	17 000	17 500	17 500
Fees	2500	3000	3000	3500	3500
Promotion	5000	5000	3000	2000	2000
Projects	–	5000	5000	2000	2000
Heritage project	5000	–	–	–	–
Capital	22 000	5000	2000	2000	2000
	197 003	189 478	190 801	195 491	204 565

adopted by the management. In a public sector facility for example, entrance to sites is usually free, with income being generated at specialist facilities such as visitor centres, cafes, shops or entrance to special events. For the private sector, visitors may be charged an overall entry fee that covers all subsequent costs (except, perhaps refreshments) or alternatively, the entrance fee may be kept low, with additional costs being incurred by the visitor for any specialist activities, such as rides, tours or talks.

Whatever the situation, however, the manager will need to ensure that the monitoring process is capable of returning the level of information required to control the management of the site. Whether or not this deals with the number of visitors to each separate element of the countryside site, to the site as a whole, or the corresponding breakdown of money spent per head will vary from site to site.

3.3.6 Summary

The business plan will act as a detailed source of information and prediction/forecast to back-up the proposals within the management plan. The need for a business plan will depend upon the requirements of the manager, and in some circumstances there will not be a need for a separate plan at all. However, the content of the business plan should be included within the body of the management plan where no separate document is prepared.

The Consultative Committee of Hadrians Wall produced a strategy for the wall, which was in essence a formative management plan (Countryside Commission, 1984).

The main elements of the study were: identifying the key components of the Wall and its 'environment'; stating aims for each of these components; developing strategies for these components/aims, based on survey information; creating an overall interpretive strategy for the Wall.

The components that were identified as critical to the integrity of the Wall were: the main sites along the Wall; the Wall itself; the landscape surrounding the Wall; the visitors and their needs; the need for information.

Objectives set for each of these components are firm and measureable, for example:

- On site interpretations should be provided for all sites open to the public.
- A scheme should be prepared for signposting pedestrian routes from the main transport modes to the Wall.
- A leaflet giving information about the 'whole wall' should be published by the three County Councils.

In order to meet these objectives, the Consultative Committee which originally had over 30 members was complemented by a Management Committee and a project officer working eventually on the key components identified in the strategy.

Figure 3.6 The strategy for Hadrians Wall: a case study. From the Countryside Commission (1984).

3.4 FURTHER CONSIDERATIONS

The management plan and the business plan do not exist in isolation and neither should the site owners or managers seek to prepare development plans or management proposals in isolation. Figure 3.7 shows a simplified but none the less useful mode for describing the total environment – physical, social and economic – within which a countryside recreation site operates. The site manager can have almost complete control over some issues, such as marketing policies or styles of interpre-

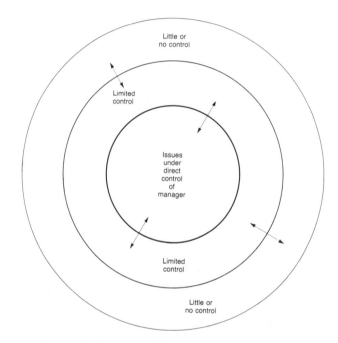

Figure 3.7 Spheres of influence model.

tation. There will be other issues over which the site management can exert some influence, but cannot completely control, such as the allocation of funds from a larger parent organization, or land designation by a local or national government organization. Finally, there are many factors which cannot be influenced by site managers, but which still have an important bearing upon the operation of the recreation site. These wider factors will include issues such as the bank interest rate or national or international attitudes towards the natural environment.

The foregoing discussion on management and business planning has inevitably concentrated upon the factors which the manager can influence. This section concentrates upon the major influencing factors that lie, at least partly, outside the direct control of the countryside recreation site management.

3.4.1 The planning system

Most countryside recreation sites will be located within an area covered by one or more elements of the local or national planning systems. This system includes the Town and Country Planning process of Local and

Structure Plans and also includes wider national contexts for countryside recreation. Thus, for example, a countryside recreation site may be located within an Area of Outstanding Natural Beauty or a National Park, as defined in the 1949 National Parks and Access to the Countryside Act. This will have a major influence upon the types of design that need to be incorporated in management plans. Similarly, if a countryside recreation site contains a Site of Special Scientific Interest (SSSI) this too will influence what activities can take place upon the land.

The Local and Structure Plan system (or, in Metropolitan areas, the Unitary Development Plan process) identifies land use across most of Britain. Countryside recreation usually represents one of the 'permitted uses' of urban fringe or rural areas covered by such plans (Countryside Commission, 1987b).

Again, this brings with it constraints and opportunities. Furthermore, it is a process which can be influenced to a certain extent by the site management as the creation of any local or national policy is open to public consultation and amendment as a legal requirement of the process. It is critical, therefore, that a countryside recreation site be seen as falling into a wider land use framework. This framework is in itself a complex structure, which will need to be prioritized if the manager of the individual site is not to spend too much time simply trying to understand the wider picture.

3.4.2 Grant regimes

For the private, voluntary sector and public providers of countryside recreation sites, finding resources – predominantly money – to support the provision will always form an important part of the work. An important element of this income for the site will inevitably come from outside grant aid. This grant aid can cover most types of work associated with countryside recreation. Forester (1989) estimates that some £182 million per annum is distributed for 'environmental purposes' throughout the United Kingdom. This flow of money covers all the possible combinations, from charitable trusts that support private sector initiatives, to government bodies that support charitable trusts, and private companies that offer assistance to schools, community groups or charitable organizations.

The criteria attached to most of these grants are drawn up by the awarding organization and to this extent cannot be influenced by site staff. However, in drawing up business or management plans the manager will need to make reference to the availability or otherwise of any grant aid and support for the provision of countryside recreation.

3.4.3 Location

Whilst the location of the park or recreation site is an issue that needs to be covered within the management plan, it does have significant implications for many management decisions, and warrants further brief discussion. The location of the site will not only affect the physical characteristics of the area, and hence, its ecological and landscape qualities, it will also produce certain visitor characteristics simply because the site is located near to (or indeed, remote from) certain groups of potential visitor. The use patterns of an urban fringe site will be markedly different from those of a more remote country park. Thus, the location of a park *vis-à-vis* its most immediate source of potential visitors will have an impact on the type of facility that eventually develops. With the best will in the world, a manager cannot develop a viable educational resource if most of the on-site rangers spend their time trying to stop fly tipping or illegal use of motorcycles.

The relationship between recreation site characteristics and local population is stressed in Tourism and Recreation Research Unit Report No. 44 (Tourism and Recreation Research Unit, 1980) in which patterns of use were recorded for four parks around Glasgow. The findings revealed that 'differences in the types of user at each park were largely determined by the structure of the population in the surrounding area' and that 'the analysis supports the contention that most parks are used by people living nearby'. This suggests that the decision where to situate a countryside recreation site will, in the first instance, have a greater impact upon the use patterns than will the type of facility provided.

3.4.4 National initiatives

Any manager will need to be aware of the way that his or her particular area of responsibility is influenced by national patterns, trends and initiatives. At a commercial level, these other initiatives may form new areas of competition for the individual site manager. At a different level, managers can clearly learn from each other. Furthermore, changes at national level will invariably bring with them problems and opportunities that the manager will need to accommodate. Changes to the Countryside Commission and the Nature Conservancy Council in 1991/92, for example, affected grant regimes and some working relationships between managers and central government. Similarly, changes to the curriculum of environmental studies in schools will need to be mirrored at countryside sites if schools are an important target group. More generally, public awareness of issues such as ozone depletion or the destruction of tropical rainforests may dictate that on-site interpretation is aimed at linking these subjects to the site-specific work. Failure to do this may result in a failure to attract the interest of the visitors. As elsewhere, therefore, managers of countryside recreation sites should be aware of the changing circumstances within which they operate at a national and international level. This needs to be accommodated within the management plan wherever possible.

3.4.5 Summary

The aim of the management plan is to provide a logical framework to allow the manager to be confident that all of the necessary considerations have been accommodated within their decision-making process and that these decisions and their outcomes are monitored as a matter of course. Management planning is also a means of ensuring that, wherever necessary, the subjective assessment of either the manager or the site owners is explicitly identified. Thus, for example, the manager may feel that the educational emphasis of the site is more (or less) important than the nature conservation emphasis. Whilst this (or any other example) may not cause major conflicts in site objectives, it does give the manager the opportunity to express these objectives clearly. And, as we have seen, clear objectives are one of the prerequisites of effective management.

The scope of the management plan will vary from one site to another. Nationally important landscapes, for example, will inevitably include, as part of their framework for the management plan, national considerations and requirements for landscape protection. This will be the case in National Parks, National Scenic Areas or Areas of Outstanding Natural Beauty, for example, in which countryside recreation sites are to be developed. The manager will, therefore, need to consider carefully which pieces of information are relevant to the management plan and which are of greatest importance.

The system outlined here for developing the management plan is based on a number of systems used by the Countryside Commission, the Countryside Councils, the National Trust, and others. For this reason alone it is a valuable starting point for managers. However, there are no strict rules for developing a management plan, and it is possible that site managers may well wish to develop their own system.

The management plan must, however, be a document that leads successfully from policy to implementation. For this reason, the plan must contain details of how the proposals are to be funded, or at least an estimate of costs and whether funds can be immediately identified to cover the works. Similarly, the plan should also consider how work will

It is all too easy to forget that not only does the earth contain valuable resources above the surface, but also, possibly, beneath it too. Information about 'ancient monuments' – from mesolithic sites to industrial listed buildings – is held on the 'Sites and Monuments Record' (SMR) held by local authorities. However, it is clear that archaeological information can often only be discovered through excavation and this, in turn, often only takes place if a site is to be developed. Indeed 'developer led' archaeology is now the sort of work promoted by government.

Thus, not all the relevant historic information is necessarily held on SMR, and not all structures are well or adequately recorded. To be sure that no damage is being done, therefore, by development or indeed to be sure that a valuable interpretive opportunity is not being missed, a 'site appraisal' should form part of the management plan survey. A site appraisal is an outline assessment of the available archaeological information and a review of the likelihood of valuable sites being present.

The relevant Government agency in England is English Heritage, and in Scotland and Wales the Secretary of State through their relevant departments.

Figure 3.8 Archaeology.

be implemented and when it should be implemented. Whilst stopping short of being a detailed work programme, therefore, the management plan should be written in such a way, and contain sufficient information, to allow it to be used as a valuable working document, not simply an information gathering exercise. As Barber (1991) states 'By creating a management plan, the organisation must commit itself to a clear course of action ... it is a statement of intentions'.

Staffing | 4

4.1 INTRODUCTION

The management of any organization begins with the people in that organization. For the manager of countryside recreation sites, this clearly suggests that the environmental resource and the people entrusted to manage that resource fall within his or her remit. The scope of this responsibility for staff will vary between sites. Some small sites, perhaps managed by voluntary organizations, may well entail no more than a site manager and two or three full-time staff. On the other hand, a country estate, which includes a central house and outbuildings used for a visitor centre/shop, areas of grassland, woodland and water, and also areas of working estate will involve a wide range of staff.

Similarly the type of work undertaken by the staff will also vary. A public authority country park may rely heavily upon the interpretive and human skills of a countryside ranger. Conversely, the upland estates managed by the National Trust, for example, require a high degree of practical work to maintain the landscape and ecological fabric of the estate. The role of the staff will, thus, vary from one site to another.

Finally, the status of the staff will also differ. As well as directly paid and supervised employees, the manager may also be involved with contractual labour, most often on larger capital projects. Furthermore, it is increasingly the case that members of the general public want to become directly involved with the management of their environment. For this reason, the site manager will need to be able to supervise and accommodate the justified demand for 'hands-on' experience from the public. This voluntary involvement will, in itself, vary from a casual one-off task to a more formalized, long-standing commitment.

The manager must, therefore, be able to identify not only the workload requirements from staff, but also be able to work with a wide range of types of workforce.

4.2 STAFFING AND THE MANAGEMENT PLAN

The overall framework for all of the above-mentioned considerations for staff must inevitably come from the management plan. The management objectives and the prescription will require implementation. For this reason, staff structures should be linked to these objectives. Where the interpretation of the site is involved, for example, responsibility of this will need to be allocated to suitable members of staff; rangers, schools liaison workers, educationalists or professional interpreters, for example. Where practical objectives are of greater importance, the need for rangers may be superseded by the requirement for estate or manual workers.

The countryside site may have a significant importance for the local community. This significance may be because of historical reasons (where the site was central to community life or events) or for more contemporary reasons (because it has always been seen as an area used for informal recreation, for example, on the urban fringe). For these reasons and because of the rising importance of environmental issues, *per se*, the manager will also have identified these factors in the management plan. Correspondingly, voluntary activity on, and involvement with, the countryside site will form a feature of its management.

This chapter reviews the elements of staffing a countryside recreation site. This includes the principles of staffing, the areas of responsibility of the staff, the type of staff and involvement by the public.

4.3 PRINCIPLES OF STAFFING

The process of staffing an organization to meet stated aims and objectives is seldom, if ever, as simple as appointing new staff to new posts with a limitless supply of money. In most situations, staff will already be in post and may indeed have been partly involved with producing the new, or most recent, management plan. Furthermore, resources rarely match the total requirements of the organization.

In these circumstances, the manager should be aware of the need to manage a changing staffing environment as well as a natural environment which is also changing. Figure 4.1 shows how the various elements with which the site manager deals intermesh. Management of change, balancing the numerous demands required of the manager is a skill in itself.

Notwithstanding the range of situations within which the countryside site manager will operate, there are a number of key principles which

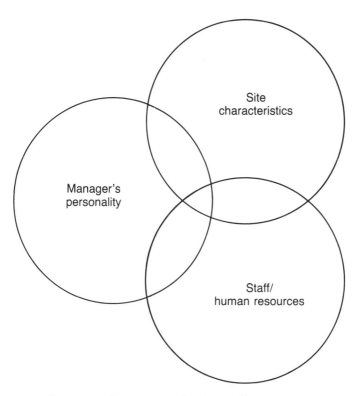

Figure 4.1 Influences on the manager's decision-making process.

underlie the process of staffing an organization. These have been identified by Torkildsen (1986).

- Train and deploy: recognize that the way that staff are trained and deployed affects results.
- Study legislation, principles and structures: understand unity of command, logical assignment and span of control.
- Create formal structures. Provide for cleanliness of authority and chains of command.
- Permit informal structures. Recognize informal structures and their importance to essential cross-communications. In doing so, accept bypassing of chains of command.
- Present sound proposals. Staffing proposals which identify essential levels, responsibilities and roles are needed.
- Create team management. Recognize the benefits of working as a well coordinated team, rather than a group of individuals.

- Avoid rigid line structures. Consider alternative methods to meet various situations. Structures must be tailor-made to suit the services to be provided.
- Make conditions flexible. The complexity, hours and patterns of work of a countryside service make flexibility important.
- Construct departments and decentralize. Divide work out into logical units or sections and identify their functions. Identify the tasks and responsibilities attached to each post.
- Start with essential staff. When providing a new service or new part to an existing service, start only with essential staff.
- Consider alternative systems for employing staff – volunteers or trusts, for example. Discussion with trade unions may be necessary to explain the need for community involvement.
- Use structures as means not ends. Staff structures must be used but if not appropriate should be amended.

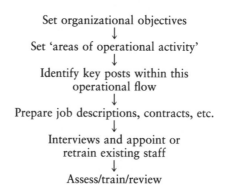

Set organizational objectives
↓
Set 'areas of operational activity'
↓
Identify key posts within this
operational flow
↓
Prepare job descriptions, contracts, etc.
↓
Interviews and appoint or
retrain existing staff
↓
Assess/train/review

Figure 4.2 The staffing process.

Figure 4.3 shows a possible staff structure for a countryside recreation site, with several of the above principles incorporated. There is a logical chain of command; areas of responsibility can be clearly identified; volunteers and full-time workers both have a role within the system; team identity can be built by each section head, and the staff structure can, if necessary, be adapted.

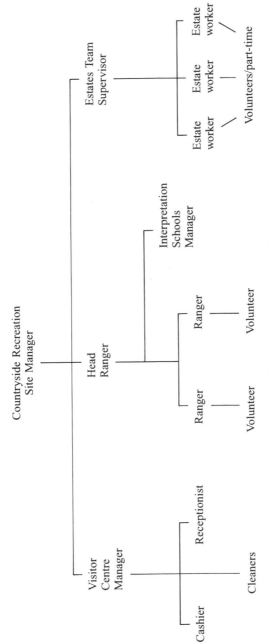

Figure 4.3 Possible staff structure for countryside recreation site.

Figure 4.4 Formal gardens require clear decisions about the staff needed to manage them – as indeed does any resource.

4.4 TYPES OF STAFF

The relationship of staff to the employing organization can vary, but for the countryside manager, the three most important types of staff are: volunteers; contract workers; and direct employees. Each of these has advantages and disadvantages in the type, amount and quality of work that they can provide.

4.4.1 Volunteers

People volunteer for a wide variety of reasons, and volunteers can be found in many areas of work. Within the countryside and environment movement in general, however, volunteer involvement is particularly important. This is partly for historical reasons because early environmental policies and acts were framed largely as a result of initiatives and pressures from voluntary groups (Lowe and Goyder, 1983). More recently, voluntary involvement has been actively encouraged on many countryside sites because it represents a good way of helping people to share and understand their own environment. A simpler explanation is that people like planting trees and creating ponds!

However, before volunteers work on countryside sites in whatever capacity, the manager has to understand fully why the volunteers are seeking to become involved or why the involvement is being encouraged. Unless the aims are clear, the involvement of volunteers is bound to fail. 'We regret the tendency of some volunteer users, especially some of those delegated to supervise the tasks, to regard volunteers as cheap labour, often accompanied by the tendency to overestimate the skills or capacity of volunteers' (Countryside Commission, 1980b).

The manager must, therefore, be aware of why volunteers wish to work: is it an educational experience; is it to learn a skill; is it to have fun; or is it to contribute, in a small way, to protecting the environment? In truth it will be many or all of these reasons. Similarly, different types of groups will also have very different thresholds of boredom – primary school children will not be very enthusiastic about an endless litter-pick, for example.

The involvement of volunteers needs careful planning, with several key stages.

1. Identifying relevant tasks: suitable tasks for volunteers will include interesting and varied work, such as tree planting, waymarking, fencing, hedging, rangering and staffing visitor centres (Shell UK, 1986).
2. Planning the task: as volunteers cannot be expected to apply the same professional standard as employees, their work load needs to be carefully planned by the manager.
3. Organizing the task: similarly, the daily organization of the work to be undertaken needs to be managed for the volunteers.
4. Training and supervision: where appropriate, the volunteers will require training. Where a greater reliance is on volunteers, a larger amount of training will be necessary. Indeed, for some volunteers, the quality of training that they will receive may be the best form of 'payment' that they require.

Given these controls, the voluntary input of time can bring beneficial results to the manager; communities will respect the environment more, people can develop a closer involvement with sites and practical work can be achieved, albeit at a lower level of quantity. Standards, however, need not drop; it has been shown, for example, that trees planted by volunteers and professional staff survive at equal rates if correct supervision is given to volunteers (Countryside Commission, 1986).

Carefully managed, therefore, the public can hold a valuable place within the process of countryside site management, especially in Local Authority or voluntary sector operations.

4.4.2 Employees

Staff employed by, and directly managed by, the owners of the sites represent the backbone of any organization. For this reason, the greatest investment of time, training and management expertise should be devoted to their development. The skills necessary to manage personnel and create a harmonious work team represent an art in themselves. Many of the key elements are discussed in section 4.3 and these must be mastered by the manager if the site is to succeed. What must concern us here, however, are the practical considerations of employee management.

Employment review is a method of continually ensuring that employees are aware of their role and function within the organization, that they are confident in all areas of work that are expected of them, and that their own work and personal objectives are being met through the job. It is a proactive way of working towards confidence and enjoyment as well as meeting organizational goals. An hour/hour and a half interview once or twice a year is a small investment, but invaluable. The review is not tied to pay awards or promotional suitability – assessment is a different activity altogether.

Figure 4.5 Employment review.

The manager will be responsible, possibly through a line subordinate, for developing the work programme of the employees. The scale of this work programme will vary, depending upon the nature of work involved and the level of command involved in programming. Estate workers, for example, may only want a weekly programme, whereas a ranger may require a monthly programme. Whatever the timescale, however, the basic prerequisite is that work is pre-planned. The original source of information for this pre-planning is the management plan; this will provide overall team objectives and individual objectives for the sections within the overall management system.

The advantages of working with employees directly can be summarized as follows.

- The manager has day-to-day access to a team of workers who will provide the core service for the countryside site.
- A full year's work programme can be developed, but flexibility can also be allowed for should the need arise.

- A continual presence of estate workers, rangers or other staff can often be a boost to users. If they see a continuous presence, they too begin to feel respect for the site.
- A regular team can begin to gain a feel for the site and develop the necessary practical and other skills to suit the characteristics of the environment.
- The manager has direct line control over the workings of the team.
- Once the salaries of the staff have been secured within budgets, the cost of any work or development will be for materials only.

It is difficult to imagine how a countryside recreation site could operate on an economic basis without core staff. However, in the private and public sectors alike, recent trends are towards contracting out most of the services, including estate or grounds maintenance, catering and shop facilities. None the less, there will still be a need to maintain a directly employed workforce of at least minimal size, if only to supervise the contracts. However, the nature of countryside recreation, and the complexity of some of the ecosystems within which that recreation takes place suggest that the degree to which the work of the manager can be contracted out is limited.

Of equal importance, particularly to the staff, are the health and safety considerations. These are detailed in section 8.4. For the staff issues under discussion here, the relevance of the heath and safety legislation is that the manager, as the agent of the employer will be responsible for ensuring that the overall health and safety of the operation meets the legal requirements. Not only is this the case for employees, but also for volunteers and contractors (as well as visitors and even trespassers!). Arrangements need to be made to ensure that the practical standards on-site, working procedures, and insurance and contracts are all legal and binding. Section 4.7 explores these obligations further.

4.4.3 Contract workers

As intimated above, some countryside managers may seek to use contract labour for a variety of reasons, often with different contracts operating for different areas of work.

Issuing and managing contracts is a profession in itself. The professional training of architects, engineers, landscape architects and many others is geared towards understanding and dealing with contract procedures. For this reason, the countryside manager should seek professional advice before entering into binding contracts, unless he or she has this expertise to hand.

At a practical level, contract workers can best be employed on single, capital construction schemes, such as developing a new car park, or planting new areas of woodland. Similarly, areas of the site that can be isolated either managerially or geographically can be contracted out. Thus, for example, cafes, site shops or open farms can be managed, under contract, separately from the main facility.

The problems with this are clear. Ensuring overall integrity of the provision, the quality of the service, the protection of the landscape and wildlife importance of the site and the balance between the contracts are, in themselves, difficult tasks. For this reason, countryside sites have tended to operate mainly with direct employees and only one subcontract for on-going management, usually catering.

For capital, construction or landscaping projects, however, the situation is somewhat simpler, and new developments that form part of the management plan can easily and conveniently be undertaken by contractors. Indeed, there are few, if any, areas of work that are undertaken within countryside recreation sites that could not be carried out by contractors: from cleaning out the toilets to surveying and managing important wildlife habitats, the manager could, if required, contract out the work.

A major consideration when issuing contracts is, therefore, the quality and standards that the manager expects from the source or habitat/landscape management. Here again, the management plan should offer guidelines, but individual contracts should contain reference to the quality of workmanship, the performance of the items under contract and any

Offer and acceptance	An offer must be clearly made and unconditionally accepted.
Intention	Both parties must show their desire to enter into a contract.
Capacity	Both or all parties must be legally capable of performing their function within the contract.
Consent	Consent to enter the contracts must not be made by fraud, duress, etc.
Legality	The contracts must be made within the law, and the objective of the contracts must also be legal.
Possibility	Contracts made to undertake tasks which are impossible are invalid.
Consideration	Each party must contribute something in exchange for the other promise.

Figure 4.6 Elements of a contract.

other details felt, by the manager, to be of relevance. This information is usually held within the full documentation that accompanies the terms of contract (Clamp, 1989).

4.4.4 Other workers

There are other types of staff that may be considered by the site manager. These have various characteristics which fall between the three types of staff identified here.

Given within 13 weeks of starting work, stating:
- Employer's name
- Employee's name
- Date and commencement/job title
- Pay and payment intervals
- Hours of work
- Entitlement of holidays, including public holidays
- Sickness procedures
- Pension arrangements
- Length of notice – entitlement
- Disciplinary and grievance procedures.

Figure 4.7 Contracts of employment: contents of a written contract.

Part-time staff can be employed to overcome peak periods of demand, an important factor in any countryside site. Peak demand usually being summer and weekends (not surprisingly). Part-time staff can also be useful to undertake occasional work, and to provide a link between volunteers and full-time staff.

Trainees are the next generation of countryside managers. For this reason alone they should, if at all possible, be encouraged within the organization. The trainees could possibly be year-out students or people who have just left full-time education and are working towards professional or craftsman status. The responsibility of the manager is, therefore, to provide the necessary training environment to allow the individual, and the organization, to develop.

Government sponsored employment schemes have in the past been referred to as Community Programme, Youth Opportunities or Employment Training. Recent thinking is that such schemes should aim to provide good quality re-training for those on the schemes. Should the manager choose, therefore, to pursue this line of staffing, it brings with it a responsibility to train. As with volunteers, government sponsored employment schemes do not represent a cheap source of labour, and so the reasons for employing the staff should be carefully understood.

4.4.5 Compulsory competitive tendering

The process of compulsory competitive tendering (CCT) applies to Local Authorities and was introduced through the Housing and Local Government Act 1988. The objective of the act was to open up Local Authority services to external competition, and one of the services identified under the CCT law was grounds maintenance. Within this context, country parks and other similar resources were specifically included within the legislation. As a consequence, the management of most Local Authority facilities could now well lie with external contractors. In any event, the system of controlling the implementation programme is increasingly through contractual arrangements. As a result, managers need to be more and more specific about the details of site management so that bills of quantities, specifications and contract documents can be drawn up. This may affect the potential for employing an on-site estate team or the amount of practical work such a team can undertake (section 4.5 below, for example). Sayers (1990) gives a comprehensive guide to the process of CCT as it effects all maintenance programmes of parks, not just informal countryside sites.

4.4.6 Summary

The manager of a countryside recreation site can employ, or allow, a wide range of staff on the site. On one hand, volunteers and community groups that wish to become involved in the shaping of their environment and cannot be truly considered as staff. On the other hand, contractors who are tightly controlled over timing, quality and provision of services and materials. The manager must, therefore, match the requirements of the management plan with the existing and available sources of manpower, and also seek to meet wider community objectives as well.

4.5 AREAS OF RESPONSIBILITY

Countryside recreation sites vary considerably. Correspondingly, the jobs that need to be undertaken by staff also vary. The basic rule of clearly allocating responsibility for areas of work is, therefore, important. There are four broad areas of responsibility, which for the sake of clarity can be discussed separately. These are: administration; estate work; range and interpretation; and specialist tasks.

4.5.1 Administration

The role of the administration is to handle the financial and organizational elements of the site management. Thus, the ordering of materials, the payment of salaries and wages, routine personnel issues and ensuring that the site and staff are suitably insured are all tasks that can be considered as administrative.

It is inevitable that the need for a specialist administration section or a member of staff may not arise in all cases. Where the site is part of a larger organization, for example, the administrative back-up may be provided from a central system. Alternatively, on a small site, the manager may be required to handle all administrative details, or the various members of staff may be required to undertake their own administrative duties. In any one of these three situations the direct responsibility of the manager will be different. However, managers must not only be aware of the procedures themselves, but also ensure that all other staff know these procedures.

If for example, rangers are expected to order materials themselves, they clearly require budgetary responsibility. This must be properly understood by all concerned. Indeed, responsibility for budgets and expenditure is one of the most important within any organization, and delegation must be carefully considered. However, ultimate responsibility will still lie with the manager.

Other administrative duties, such as report writing, personnel management and organization of events are less onerous, but still important for the running of the site. Some of these, and others, can effectively be delegated to other staff where a central administrative section is absent or where the manager sees it as being advantageous. In most single sites, the administrative duties will usually be undertaken by the manager and other section or team heads. Only on large sites will a specialist administrative team be justified.

4.5.2 Estate work

Any countryside recreation site will require estate management. By the definition used within this text, any site on which the quality of the land itself forms a major element of the value of the site will need regular maintenance and development. We saw in the previous section that major works can sometimes be undertaken through contractors. However, in many situations it may be appropriate to have a team of estate workers whose responsibility it is to carry out regular and routine management.

The actual workload of the estate team will vary from site to site, as

Figure 4.8 The nature of the site will, to a large extent, determine the skills needed from an estate's or management team.

the nature of, and characteristics of, the site may vary. An area of woodland, for example, will require a different set of skills to an area of grassland. Similarly, an upland limestone area may require from the estate teams skills in dry stone wall construction, whereas a lowland area may involve pond and wetland management in its upkeep.

The site manager will need to determine the best system for managing the physical fabric of the entire site, and as we have seen this will usually be a mixture of paid staff, contractors and volunteers. Included within this mix might also be the alternative of leasing out land for management by a third party – perhaps a farmer to use some of the site's grassland for grazing his or her sheep or cattle. The implications of this for the estate team is that only part of the overall land management process will be part of their responsibility.

Notwithstanding this, the estate team will require a relatively standard set of core skills, which will be called upon time and again. These include: fencing; footpath/step construction; stile erection; tree planting and management; hedgerow and stone wall management; and pond and wetland management. The level of skill required in each of these areas of work will depend upon the nature of the site. In each case, however, the estate workers will need to work in a sympathetic and often traditional manner in order to protect the landscape and natural history integrity of the site, as well as opening the area for countryside recreation.

The British Trust for Conservation Volunteers has long been involved in the management of the physical environment and has produced guidelines for the sympathetic construction and maintenance of a range of natural and man-made landscapes. This includes hedgerows, woodlands, footpaths and many of the other elements of estate management (British Trust for Conservation Volunteers, various years).

The day-to-day management of the estate team will usually fall to a team supervisor, although, on small sites in particular, this could also be the overall site manager. The actual workload of the team will be developed, which pulls together the management plan, the skills of the team, work priorities, the type of work and the time of year.

Where both an estate team and a team of rangers are present on the same site it is vital that clear areas of responsibility are determined (as, indeed, it is in all circumstances and for all posts). This is particularly important here because it is often rangers, because of the nature of their job, who first notice the need for a particular piece of work. It has to be clear, therefore, who will actually repair, say, a broken stile and how any orders or instructions to carry out the work will be made. On countryside sites it is crucial that repairs are carried out quickly and efficiently. This is because, in the eyes of the untrained public, the only difference between an un-managed and a managed site may well be the quality of the fences or stiles, or the state of repair of picnic tables, for example. If countryside managers are to engender a respect for the countryside in the general public, they themselves must be able to reflect their own respect by being able to repair and manage the land quickly and sympathetically. In many ways, this efficiency lies at the heart of good countryside management, so a clear understanding of site responsibility is important.

4.5.3 Rangers

The countryside ranger was first given legal recognition in Britain through the 1949 National Parks and Access to the Countryside Act. National Park Wardens (as they were then called) were envisaged as people who would 'secure compliance with by-laws'; the role of the ranger was originally one of surveillance of the use made of National Parks. With the passing of the 1968 Countryside Act, enhancement of the visitors' enjoyment, conservation of the site through management practices, protection of the visitors and surveillance, are now all seen as the role of the ranger (Countryside Commission, 1979b). Furthermore, the land upon which the ranger can legally operate has also been extended. Thus, rangers now operate in a positive, interpretive way on public and private land and land owned by voluntary sector organizations.

The work of the ranger is, therefore, 'people orientated' with the ranger dealing with visitors to the countryside on a one-to-one and group basis. Increasing the enjoyment of visitors to the countryside can be undertaken in a number of ways: through guided walks, through informal contacts with visitors, by providing information and by controlling antisocial behaviour. This interpretive role of the ranger may also take him or her outside the actual countryside site into schools, community groups and evening classes, for example. The manager should assess carefully whether this is a desired part of the site provision. An objective of the Countryside Commission (Countryside Commission, 1987b) for the year 2000 is to include rangers in linking countryside recreation sites with the 'wider countryside'. However, the site manager may feel that site-based work is, initially at least, more important.

With a more interpretive role to play, the surveillance and practical work of rangers has become secondary. None the less, they remain important. A knowledge of countryside law is, therefore, critical for the ranger (Parkes, 1983, for example). Similarly, although some practical schemes will be undertaken through an estate team or contract workers, the rangers are in an ideal situation to undertake small repairs to stone walls, fences and stiles. For this reason, allowance should be made within the ranger's work programme to do this small-scale work. The rangers also have a role to play in supervising voluntary work on site. Thus, the ranger will need to have at least a working knowledge of some practical skills in order to help community or school groups learn through practical work.

Thus, the ranger lies at the centre of the management process and the manager should allocate resources accordingly. A structured ranger service, with a senior or head ranger having responsibility for full-time, part-time and voluntary rangers is ideal.

4.5.4 Specialist tasks

The number of specialist tasks that the manager requires of his or her staff will clearly depend upon many factors; the nature of the site, the

Figure 4.9 The handling of money, machinery and managing a building all require staff that are trained to look after the complex range of issues.

aims of the management, the objectives of the manager, and visitor requirements, for example.

The types of specialist staff that are often required by countryside site managers might include the following:

- *Receptionist* for work in visitor centres and information points. These staff will need to deal with a wide range of people and have access to a large amount of information.
- *Cashiers* where shops are included within the organization of the site, staff who are able to deal with cash transactions will be needed. As well as interpersonal skills, these staff will also require various levels of financial management ability.
- *Catering staff* a common feature of many countryside sites is that they cater for the refreshments required by visitors. This may range from snack food to a full restaurant facility. In any event, some specialist catering staff may be required.
- *Cleaners* where the public have access to buildings and toilets, it is

inevitable that these areas (and others) will need cleaning. This may be of such a scale that cleaners will need to be employed.

Any of these specialist staff, and others that may be required, can be employed directly or through contracts. One of the key roles of management will be to determine the best mix of contractors, direct employees and community involvement on the site in order to meet the objectives.

It must be remembered, however, that countryside recreation sites are managed to provide people with an enjoyable recreational experience and to protect the environment. The balance struck through the various forms of employee status will not, inevitably, be the least expensive. A lot of resources on countryside sites inevitably go into the personnel required, and as most managers will be aware, employing people can be expensive! However, if the personal interpretive element of the countryside experience is to be provided, these staff need to be present on-site.

4.6 PERSONNEL MANAGEMENT

The site manager will inevitably be faced with managing people, both directly and indirectly. This needs skill and special understanding if it is to be successful, because an almost accidental collection of people does not automatically become a team unless energy and time is devoted to this end. Simply sitting back and having 'an open door policy' seldom, if ever, works. Managing people takes time and patience.

It is impossible to cover all the relevant personnel issues here, or even to cover the broad details. As with everything else that the manager must face, the need for detailed knowledge about personnel and related legal matters must be balanced against the other requirements of the manager and the site. Some brief pointers to the main topics include the following elements:

- All staff should have contracts of employment, job descriptions (based on the requirements of the management and/or business plan) and conditions of employment, including health and safety policies, disciplinary and grievance procedures and other policies.
- By employing staff, the manager and the organization that he or she represents becomes liable for the person's actions and so adequate and reasonable training and information needs to be provided to ensure, as far as possible, that these liabilities can be enacted.
- A group of individuals does not automatically become a team that works towards a common goal. Similarly, the existence of a good

team spirit does not mean that individuals do not have their own personal requirements or work objectives. A commitment to team building and some form of individual employment review helps to balance these elements.

- Systems of good practice exist for personnel management. In large organizations, written policies will already exist, but for smaller or newer ventures disciplinary and grievance procedures, management culture, training programmes and policies on career development may need to be established. Help can be brought in and guidance sought from consultants, professional bodies or ACAS, for example.

FWAG officers are responsible for advice, guidance and information to the farming community, often across several counties. A training strategy was developed to help staff become more competent in core, organizational and managerial/personal skills.

This was based upon:

Assessment	using questionnaires and interviews;
Review	of existing training provision;
Workshop	of staff and external agencies to review priorities, and develop a structure;
Recommendation	including induction training, coaching, staff training budgets, personal training requirement;
Review	of whole policy and individual requirements.

Figure 4.10 Training strategy: case study of Farming Wildlife Advisory Group (FWAG) officers.

4.7 EMPLOYMENT LAW

There is a plethora of Acts of Parliament which define the relationship between employers and their staff from the point at which they are recruited to when they leave. Furthermore, there is a wide range of case law and agreements which further define what is 'reasonable' in employment relationships.

The manager will not usually be the employer, but will often be the agent of the employer, charged with responsibility for enacting or ensuring compliance with the relevant legislations. This ranges from health and safety legislation (Health and Safety at Work Act 1974) through sexual and racial discrimination (Race Relations Act 1976 and Sex Discrimination Acts 1975 and 1986, for example) to payment (Wages Act 1986, or Equal Pay Act 1970) maternity benefits and employees' general rights (Employment Act 1980, for example) or Trade Union membership (Employment Act 1990).

Larger organizations will usually have a section or department dealing with the legal aspects of employment, or this might be part of the broader 'personnel' function. Smaller organizations will not have such a luxury, so the manager will not have access to ready expert information or specific policies relating to areas of law.

Several organizations exist to help managers ensure that they adhere to the requirements of employment law, and that their own policies (either written or *de facto*) do not transgress these laws. The most appropriate for many managers, where organizational information is not available, are ACAS, the Commission for Racial Equality or from texts such as Croners (1991).

4.8 SUMMARY

Staffing a countryside recreation site inevitably involves a fine balance between providing the impression of a natural and peaceful environment and providing a well-managed and well-interpreted site. On the one hand, people want to feel less constrained in the countryside than they do, say, in an urban park. On the other hand, many people still require some assistance in enjoying the countryside. This personal element of countryside management is equally as important for the manager as the practical aspects of environmental management. Managing 'people and place' is integral to countryside management.

Facilities and opportunities | 5

5.1 INTRODUCTION

For most people, the countryside represents an opportunity to get away from it all and is an informal and natural place in which to take recreation. Table 7.1 shows the reasons why one large sample of people visited the countryside. The provision of facilities within countryside recreation sites, therefore, represents a balance between providing for this desire for informality and providing suitable facilities for some of the visitors who may require more than the simple pleasure of access to attractive countryside.

The site itself will dictate the suitability of certain types of activity, with natural history, landscape and archaeological considerations being important constraints on the development of facilities. It is this balance that is central to the debate that surrounds proposals to extend provision for skiing in the Scottish Highlands or the building of holiday homes in National Parks. For the site manager, the need for balance is no less important.

An equally valid determinant of the recreational provision on country-side sites is the expectations and desires of the visitor and potential visitors. The Tourism and Recreation Research Unit (1980), for example, showed that patterns of existing use of four countryside and urban fringe sites in and around Glasgow determined the nature of the provision within the site. This existing use was in turn determined by local, historical, cultural and socio-economic parameters.

The provision of visitor facilities will be determined by the management plan. Where a site needs to be self-financing, for example, there will clearly be a need for facilities which generate money. However, those need not necessarily be intrusive or unsympathetic, and the manager here has a key role to play in balancing financial and other considerations. Where financial constraints are not as critical (Table 3.1, for example) the provision of recreational facilities and opportunities can be slightly more flexible, and the requirements of the natural environment can be more central to proposals.

This chapter discusses some of the commoner types of provision that countryside managers develop in their sites. The analysis does not include the more obvious facilities such as toilets or car-parks/bicycle parks. This is not because they are not important, as this is clearly not the case. These facilities are, however, common to most recreation sites, and are not characteristic or unique to the countryside recreation site. The countryside manager has a number of types of provision of which he or she must be specifically aware. Six such areas of provision are discussed, namely: informal facilities, formal play areas, visitor centres, site shops, special displays, and sports activities.

5.2 INFORMAL FACILITIES

Informal facilities within the countryside provide for the basic use of the countryside. At its most informal, a site may consist of no more than an area of countryside, with paths crossing it to allow for degrees of public access. This simple level of provision is most appropriate for areas that seek to provide for people who want as natural an environment as possible: indeed, a truly 'natural' site would not have any paths at all. Such a site may either be a sensitive landscape or ecosystem where intensive pressure cannot be encouraged, or may be a relatively durable site but where, for reasons of management intensive use is not wanted; on local nature reserves, for example.

Footpaths require careful planning. This is clearly needed to lessen the impact on the countryside, to ensure that routes are provided in places that the public actually want them, and, if necessary, to divert people away from sensitive or dangerous areas. The British Trust for Conservation Volunteers (1983) outline the process of planning for and developing a footpath network within the countryside. The footpath development process breaks down into a number of key areas.

- Planning: reviewing and analysing the impact that the footpath will have on the site and the patterns of preferred and required use by the public.
- Preparation: draining, cleaning and otherwise creating a route through which the path will pass.
- Surfacing: surfaces should not only be environmentally sympathetic,

Figure 5.1 Simply providing a path that is accessible to all, including the disabled, opens up immense recreational opportunities.

but also stand up to the anticipated levels of use. In some areas, 'artificial' surfaces may not be appropriate at all.
- Ancillary requirements: this will include bridges, stiles, steps and revetment.
- Waymarking: to ensure the proper use of the footpath system, it may be necessary to mark the path, although this obviously detracts from the natural feel of the countryside.

Paths, therefore, represent the simplest and most informal level of provision. There are, however, other types of facility that can enhance the public's visit to a recreation site without detracting too much from the countryside nature of the site.

Picnic tables, seats and focal points, fall into this category. Pieces of suitably designed furniture, like seats or picnic tables not only extend the range of informal opportunities for visitors, but also begin to influence the way that visitors use and move about within the site. Similarly, pieces of woodland sculpture or existing features such as follies or old quarries begin to provide variety of experience for the visitors, thus

Figure 5.2 Play areas act as magnets to children and their parents, and on some countryside sites can act as a focus for family recreation.

increasing their enjoyment of the site. The Countryside Commission (1985b) has explored some of the interplay that exists between informal (and other) provision on a countryside recreation site, and the way that visitors use and enjoy the site.

The types of provision that might be defined as informal will vary with the site: what may be considered as informal on an urban fringe site could well be a very formal feature in a relatively remote or wild area. Even something as simple as a picnic table takes on different perspectives on different sites.

The Countryside Commission for Scotland (1981) issues a range of detailed information covering the design of many informal countryside features such as waymarks, bridges, seats, tables and gates. The Countryside Commission (1981) has also provided detailed information on informal provision for disabled people.

5.3 PLAY AREAS

Many people visit the countryside in a family or mixed age unit. Children, therefore, represent regular and enthusiastic users of the countryside. Thus, the countryside site manager must consider providing specific resources to allow and encourage children to play in and hence explore and ultimately respect the countryside.

Children play for a number of reasons (Hart, 1979) but play can be broken down into three broad elements: motor play (physical activity), social play (socializing with adults, other children and interacting) and cognitive play (learning through play). In short, children learn about life through play, the converse of which is that children play almost constantly. The countryside, therefore, represents an ideal area in which to develop life skills through play. It offers many existing natural resources, such as trees, space, water, rocks, wildlife, hills, valleys and much more.

Thus, the manager can encourage play simply by providing a variety of experiences within the site. Alternatively, the manager can provide more specific or formal facilities. These may range from a number of 'natural' but none the less exciting features (such as tree stumps, rocks or dense bushes) to much more formal adventure playgrounds.

The Countryside Commission for Scotland (1984) identifies ten types of play provision which can be accommodated on countryside sites. These can be summarized as shown below.

- Sculptural playgrounds: areas designed as a pleasing sight and an exciting area for children (and adults) to explore.
- Adventure playgrounds: usually enclosed areas where children can enjoy exciting and strenuous play.
- Creative play: where loose or modular equipment is provided for children to build, manufacture and create their own play.
- Nature areas: small, semi-natural areas where the excitement derives from contact with the natural environment.
- Children's farms: specialist areas where children can come into contact with domestic and farm animals.
- Trim-track: a smaller version of the adult trim-track: a route along which are positioned set exercises.
- Kickabout area: an open area for informal and formal games to be organized by the children or adults.
- Disabled play areas: specially designed play areas for disabled children.
- Play schemes: holiday or weekend events for children with guided or organized play.

- Display equipment: information boards or treasure trails can act as a stimulus to play and an aid to discovery.

These types of play area may overlap and several may be provided on one site. The manager must, however, be aware in all circumstances of the age, capacity and overall ability of children for whom play equipment is being provided. Not only must it fit into the environment, and the management plan, but also cater for the play, social and learning needs of children.

5.4 VISITOR CENTRES

The term visitor centre covers a wide range of buildings and construction in the countryside, and herein lies a great deal of the difficulty in developing a visitor centre. The manager must have a clear understanding of the exact purpose for a proposed visitor centre. Barrow (1988) has identified a number of reasons why a countryside manager may wish to provide a visitor centre. These include: operational needs (staff offices; stores; ranger office/centre; a workspace for repairs), customer needs (toilets; refreshments; a shelter from the rain; a shop), educational/interpretive needs (a classroom; an exhibition space; a gathering point; a centre for interpretive staff) and finally, practical needs (the need to use a redundant building, for example).

Within this list, managers must make absolutely sure that the need for the building is clearly understood, not just by themselves but also within the whole management structure. Only in this way will the visitor centre have a chance of being a success. Once the requirements of the building have been established, its design and operational needs can also be assessed. This is what Barrow terms 'working backwards'. Too often a building is constructed and various 'uses' forced upon it by the management.

Uses of a visitor centre may include: information provision (what to do, where to see it and so on), orientation points (gathering points for all visitors before they pass into the main site, and enabling them to find their directions and points of reference), interpretation (educational and interpretive materials on display, or audiovisual performances) and heritage displays (wherein a story or history is told of the site, or some part of it).

Once the manager has established the reasons for the building (and in some circumstances, a building may not be necessary at all; a point that the manager must consider), he or she must involve all the necessary individuals within the design process. This will include the architect, landscape design staff, interpretive staff and, if appropriate other staff who may use the building. Central to this process will be the architect, and the manager must be able to give the architect the appropriate, detailed brief. This brief should cover all of the items previously identified. These include the points listed below.

- The client: the organization or individual who is commissioning the design. Is it a private or public body, for example.
- The project objectives: is the project to restore a building, to provide a focus, to help in the interpretive process? These specific objectives need to be identified and, if possible prioritized.
- The market of the building: who will use the building; how will they see it? What age of people will be catered for? Will they be disabled? Visitor surveys will help to identify the market, but through providing a new facility, the visitor profile will inevitably change too.
- Site conditions: the architect will need to know the constraints of the site, such as landscape, boundaries or ecological constraints. A landscape designer will be critical in this stage of design.
- What facilities are needed: specific requirements such as toilets, offices, cafes, classroom or exhibition space need to be pointed out.
- Operations: the way that the building will operate will affect the design. Pay books, sales points, rubbish collection, rangers vans or first aid requirements may need to be accommodated.
- Funding; the project may have to be phased if funding is not secured for all of the project. Sponsors may need to be consulted.
- Timescale: the timescale of design, building and management will need to be explained to the architect.

These considerations are vital to the successful design and building of a visitor centre. Once the centre is built, the management of the building will clearly fall to the manager of the site. As we have seen, specific responsibility for the centre may or may not fall to a separate member of staff. Where the visitor centre is a base for the site ranger service and an interpretive/educational resource, it may be appropriate that the head ranger manages the centre. Where the centre houses a restaurant, the restaurant manager may also be given responsibility for managing the whole centre.

Costs for running a visitor centre will vary according to the purpose of the building, but a carefully constructed building needs to be fully staffed and equipped if it is to continue to be successful. Barrow (1988)

1. Establish the end use of the building – only in this way can the manager 'work backwards' from the end product.

2. Determine the spatial requirements of the building – formulae exist for m² per visitor/through-puts/maximum useage, etc. Identify separate rooms that will be needed.

3. Establish other requirements, such as external needs, locational requirements, landscaping constraints and others.

4. Assess running and maintenance cost if necessary, the basic requirements can be amended to reduce costs. Alternatively, revenue-generating targets will be higher (but still realistic).

5. Establish and discuss brief with architect. Be prepared to amend initial concepts, but not the 'end use'. Architects will be able to reduce costs, help with spatial/legal requirements but not necessarily the useage.

6. Engage architects and establish working brief. Prepare for launch and opening. Employ necessary staff. Plan for marketing and the ongoing management.

Figure 5.3 Development of a visitor centre.

suggests that at 1988/1989 prices, a visitor centre will cost in the order of £75 000–£80 000 per annum to run as a multifunctional resource.

5.5 SHOPS OR SALES POINTS

Much of the foregoing discussion relates to the provision of a shop or restaurant. Indeed, a shop or catering site may well be a part of the visitor centre. The manager needs to plan the development of a commercial shop or restaurant equally as carefully as the visitor centre. Similarly, the architect and other staff will need to be fully briefed before the scheme can begin to take shape.

Once the shop or sales point has been built, its management will operate in a different way from a visitor centre *per se*. Similarly a shop and a sales point will also be managed differently; the inference being that a shop is a building or at least a large room in its own right, a sales point is a much less important/intrusive resource.

Several key considerations need to be taken into account in any commercial venture that operate as part of a countryside site – shops, sales points, cafes or other facilities – where money changes hands.

First, it is important that the manager is sure that the site, or any part of it, can operate in a commercial manner. For private sector operations, this is usually of no concern. However, for a public authority or some charities, a trading operation, based on the intention to make a profit is illegal. This means that the manager must either operate the shop by proxy through a contractor or leasee, or set up a separate trading company to manage the resource.

Secondly, it is important to keep separate records for the shop. These will include not only the accounts, but also records of other costs and considerations, such as staff, electricity, rates and so on. It is also important that any revenue generated by the sales can be returned into the overall management of the site. Where there is a contractual arrangement with the site owners, rather than management, or where the site is operated by a Local Authority, this is not as straightforward as might seem likely. Proper mechanisms must, therefore, be established to allow income and expenditure transfers between the various elements of the site. In countryside recreation it is almost inevitable that some parts of the site will not make money, but others will. The manager must be able to balance these off against each other.

A further consideration is the type of atmosphere that the shop is trying to create. This atmosphere is formed by individual elements within the shop and the combination of these single elements. Thus, the products on sale in the shop, the opportunity for simply looking at the goods, and the space within the shop, all contribute to the feel of the shop as English Heritage (1980) suggest 'Get the ambience of the shop right to encourage visitors to browse and buy'.

The details of the shop may best be designed by expert staff. Where the financial success of the site depends upon sales, this is critical. Shop layout, size, design and range of stock are all points upon which specialist advice may be necessary. Shelf layout, display areas and packaging are becoming exact 'sciences', into which a lot of research time is put, predominantly by large retail chains. Whilst a countryside shop may be a little less ambitious, the lessons learned from this research are especially applicable in small shops.

Finally, cash and stock flows are skills that the shop manager will require. It is self-evident, therefore, that if staff are given added responsibility for shop or sales management additional training will be necessary. The alternative is, of course, to employ specialist staff. Similarly, staff who work within the shop, as cashiers or assistants, will require the necessary skills. It is to be expected that staff may have a range of responsibilities, and where shop staff are recruited from within existing staff, training is essential.

5.6 SPECIALIST DISPLAYS

'Specialist displays' cover a wide range of services, facilities or opportunities which might be appropriate within a countryside recreation site. The multi-use function that the countryside site fulfils dictates that certain types of specialist activity will be appropriate. Formal sports or activities are discussed in the next section. Two specific types of specialist display are discussed here, namely open farm and heritage exhibitions.

5.6.1 Open farms

It is possible that a countryside recreation site may be based upon an existing or working farm, or that a farm forms part of a larger countryside resource, as on a large country estate, for example. In these circumstances, the manager might feel it appropriate that the farm be part of the focus of the recreational experience of the site. Alternatively a countryside recreation site may start without an agricultural element, but the manager might consider that the recreational and interpretive size of the site would be greatly increased by a small collection of farm animals. In either event; it is necessary to plan the concept of an open farm carefully. The Countryside Commission (1974) identify the basic principles of developing farm open days, many of which can be transferred to the concept of a recreational site which is open permanently for public enjoyment.

Table 5.1 Age profile of visitors to farm open days

Age	Visitors (%)	Population of England and Wales (%)
0–14	34.5	24.0
15–24	8.2	15.0
25–44	31.0	24.0
45–64	21.4	24.0
65 and over	4.9	13.0

Source: Countryside Commission (1974)

To manage a farm through which the public have access, several key factors need to be assessed. These include the amount of access that will be encouraged; whether the farm is a working farm or purely for display purposes; who is to staff the farm; and what benefits the farmer or farm manager is seeking.

In order to address these and other criteria properly, the manager must address the managerial objectives for creating an open farm, and also assess the objectives of, and advantages for, the farmer, if the farm is separate from the main site management structure.

Table 5.2 (a) Visitor profiles to farm open days by socio-economic group

Socio-economic group	Visitors (%)	All economically active males in England and Wales (%)	Visitors on holiday (%)	Visitors not on holiday (%)
Employers and managers	8.4	10.7	10.8	7.5
Professional	24.8	4.6	28.5	23.3
Non-manual	31.2	17.2	37.1	28.9
Skilled manual	16.8	39.5	10.8	19.4
Semi-skilled and agri-cultural	12.4	17.7	5.1	15.5
Unskilled manual	3.7	8.1	0.8	4.9
Unclassified and non-response	2.7	2.0	6.9	0.4

Source: Countryside Commission (1974)

Table 5.2 (b) Visitor profiles to farm open days by distance travelled

Distance (km)	Visitors travelling from their homes (%)	Visitors travelling from temporary accommodation (%)
0–10	35.7	44.1
11–20	31.2	32.7
21–30	13.0	17.1
31–40	4.7	2.6
41–50	6.7	1.1
51 and over	8.5	1.8
Non-response	0.2	0.6

Source: Countryside Commission (1974)

Several objectives can be seen to result from providing an open farm:

- To provide an interesting and enjoyable experience for the public;
- To increase the visitor's understanding of farming;
- To influence the behaviour of people in the countryside through better understanding;
- To allow the agricultural community to understand the visitor's viewpoint on the countryside.

Additionally, the farm enterprise could benefit through:

Figure 5.4 A 'show farm' is popular and educational, but brings new areas of responsibility for staff and management.

- Increasing or developing sales from the farm;
- Experimenting with diverse farm management, before creating more intensive recreational opportunities;
- Contributing to a wider social event for the community, such as a village fête or a spring fair.

In order to meet these objectives, the manager should identify the type of people that the farm will seek to attract and whether they are different from the target groups of the main site. Similarly, within the open farm the manager may seek to provide a number of opportunities or facilities to serve the visitor, such as farm centres, information panels, school visits, leaflets or special events.

The scale of the farming operation will depend upon the role that it plays within the overall site, and how much of the site revenue needs to be generated through the farm.

5.6.2 Heritage displays

Heritage displays, or living history, are an increasingly popular and effective method of not only entertaining visitors to the countryside, but also of interpreting a site, particularly the cultural and human elements of the site. Heritage displays can be a permanent feature of a site, or can form one of a number of facilities and methods of interpretation used on the site. In the former case, a countryside site that has a permanent historical context will be similar to an open air museum, and the dividing line between the two types of facility becomes very blurred at this point.

Whether the heritage of a site forms a permanent or a temporary focus for a countryside site, there are a number of types of methods of involving visitors in living history (Centre for Environmental Interpretation (CEI), 1987, for example).

- Costumed guides/rangers: rangers or people leading guided walks or staff in site shops can dress in period costume and interpret/enact their life from an historic standpoint. This may be appropriate say, where a site is based around a piece of ancient woodland where the manager wishes to explain the former uses and misuses of the woodland.
- Demonstration: staged displays of ancient or old skills such as charcoal burning or hurdle making, will not only help to explain the value of the countryside skills, but will also provide the manager with a certain amount of income through the sale of produce.
- Period re-enactments: performances of plays, mock battles or cameos of historic events will add a visual spectacle and, if properly managed, help to transmit a feel for the action and an understanding of the events, and thus the site's historic or cultural significance.
- Participation: actually getting visitors to participate is a much more time-consuming and labour-intensive activity than the other examples but may ultimately lead to a greater level of understanding. The National Trust, for example, has developed a Young National Trust Theatre (Melhulish, 1987) which actively encourages participation in re-enactments on National Trust properties.

Living history, or heritage displays can form a valuable theme for a countryside recreation site, providing the landscape, ecological and other considerations are sufficiently well protected through the management plan.

Open farms and heritage displays are just two types of specialist activity that complement the work of the countryside manager. Individual managers may feel that other types of activity are appropriate, but the prerequisite of careful planning and coordination with other management objectives are equally as applicable.

5.7 FORMAL RECREATION

The countryside site manager can provide on his or her site a wide range of formal opportunities for recreation. Miles and Seabrooke (1993) suggest that an 'activity list is, without doubt, a handy tool'. Such a list can provide a check list and a prompt for ideas. In its longest form, it will contain some activities that are either ecologically or visually unacceptable, or alternatively generate ideas that are physically impossible, but where a broad assessment of possibilities is needed a list can be useful. The experienced manager will, however, be able to match site potential with possibilities. Where these constraints are pushed to their limit, it is almost inevitable that conflicting attitudes will arise. Thus, in the Cairngorms, at Lurchers Gully, the proposals to extend skiing provision brought nature conservationists and recreationalists into sharp conflict (Nature Conservancy Council, 1987).

The types of recreational provision that are commonly contained within countryside sites are discussed below.

5.7.1 Cycling

Providing routes for, or the actual facilities for the hire of cycles is, in many ways, an ideal complement to countryside site provision. Cycles are quiet, environmentally friendly, allow close contact with the natural environment and are relatively cheap. The Countryside Commission and several other environmental or countryside agencies actively promote the use of cycles in the countryside (Hudson 1978; Countryside Commission, 1980a). A basic key to successful provision for cycles is their careful integration into the infrastructure of the site. This will include: providing safe, and where necessary, separate routes for cycles; adequate waymarking; safe crossing points; and information for users and cyclists alike.

5.7.2 Horse riding

Horses are, in many ways, a similar type of opportunity to cycling, which the manager may consider. For example, both horses and cycles are permitted on bridleways, and, on a more negative note, both horses and cycles can on occasion, cause some conflict with pedestrians! However, horses are a natural part of many countryside recreation sites, and careful provision for them can be beneficial and, indeed, financially rewarding.

5.7.3 Orienteering

Some sites will be suitable for orienteering events, and the benefit of orienteering (or other similar sports, such as cross-country, or marathon events) is that provision is not a permanent feature of the site, and routes and courses can be removed as necessary, or waymarks only brought on to site on appropriate days.

5.7.4 Water sport

Where the site contains a large body of either moving or still water, the formal sports that can be provided for are as varied as land-based sports. For the manager, much of the difficulty lies in balancing the conflicting demands for use. Anglers and canoeists, for example, still do not always see eye to eye. Similarly, the use of power boats will seriously damage not only the bankside vegetation, but also the quietness of the countryside. In these and other situations the manager will need to consider whether certain activities are supportable in a countryside location and, if so whether some form of zoning may be required.

5.7.5 Field sports

Many private estates survive financially because of the revenue generated by field or estate sports. Equally, many publicly owned sites are covered by by-laws that explicitly forbid field sports or hunting. However, the arguments for and against such sports will continue. Rayston (1985) identifies ten field sports supported on the Broughton estate in Northamptonshire (and 12 other formalized leisure pursuits also supported on the estate). The field sports range from pigeon shooting to coarse angling and mink shooting.

5.7.6 Winter sports

Winter sports can provide a valuable income for many sites, and open new recreational opportunities for some people. Downhill or cross-country skiing are common in many upland areas, and the lack of good facilities means that provision can provide financial rewards. As with many sports, however, if the manager seeks to provide for these specialist activities, additional staff and/or safety requirements will need to be met.

5.7.7 Sports fields

In certain circumstances, sports areas may be considered appropriate. The manager may, for example, suggest that field games be provided for, such as football or cricket. In some sites these fields could also be used as events areas for spectator sports or countryside fêtes, for example. Under normal situations, however, field games and countryside recreation will not usually be compatible.

The above sections cover no more than a brief overview of the types of activity that the countryside manager might consider appropriate on the site. The views of the manager and the wishes of the site manager will all need to be explored in the management plan, and the suitability or otherwise of the proposed formal provision examined.

Angling	Riding
Canoeing	Running
Caving	Sailing
Climbing	Sail boarding
Golf	Sub-aqua
Hang-gliding	Swimming
Motor sports	Walking
Off-road cycling	Water skiing
Orienteering	Wildfowling

Figure 5.5 Sports and recreation in the countryside: common activities.

5.8 PUTTING IT ALL TOGETHER

The numerous activities and opportunities explored within this chapter will only rarely be found on the same countryside site. Given the underlying reason why most people visit the countryside (for peace and quiet, or to get away from it all), it is unlikely that too much activity on a site will continue to promote a countryside feel. However, even a small number of activities can provide the manager with problems. Horse riders and pedestrians for example, will come into very close contact with each other, particularly on a small site. Similarly, open farms will require a lot of additional land for grazing or exercise, for example, which will reduce the amount of open space available for walking or picnicking.

Figure 5.6 Does the site warrant a caravan or camping site? If so, where?

It is these conflicting pressures which the manager must seek to balance. This can be done, first, by providing an appropriate mix of activities and facilities which balance the requirements of the management, the visitors and the environment. Having developed this balance, the manager will then have to control the activities. This can be done through some form of spatial zoning of the site, so that the activities are kept separate if necessary. The manager can also keep activities separate over time, by say restricting angling, horse riding or use by schools to certain times or days. Furthermore, into this regular pattern of use, the manager may have to fit specialist events, such as countryside fêtes, heritage days or guided walks.

The quality of recreational experience will depend greatly upon the manager's ability to create a pleasant, countryside environment which, where appropriate, provides the visitor with information, activity and the opportunity to simply take a breath of fresh air. The balance provided will, therefore, vary from site to site and from manager to manager.

Table 5.3 Sports and recreation: rates of participation

Sport/recreation	Percentage of persons aged 16 and over participating in 4 weeks prior to interview, Great Britain			
	1977	1980	1983	1986
Outdoor				
Walking – 2 miles or more (including rambling/hiking)	17	19	19	19
Swimming	2	2	3	2
Football	3	3	3	3
Golf	2	2	2	3
Athletics – track and field (incl. jogging)	1	1	2	3
Fishing	2	2	2	2
Cycling	1	1	2	2
Tennis	1	2	1	1
Bowls	1	1	1	1
Camping/caravanning	1	1	1	1
Horse riding	1	1	1	1
Cricket	1	1	1	1
Field sports	1	–	–	–
Sailing (excl. windsurfing)	–	–	–	–
Rugby	–	–	–	–
Field studies	1	–	–	–
Climbing/potholing	–	–	–	–
At least one outdoor activity				
excluding walking	15	16	17	18
including walking	28	30	31	32
Indoor				
Snooker/billiards/pool	6	7	8	9
Swimming	5	6	7	9
Darts	9	7	7	6
Keep fit/yoga	1	2	3	3
Squash	2	2	3	2
Badminton	2	2	2	2
Table tennis	2	2	1	1
Bowls/tenpin	1	1	1	2
Gymnastics/athletics	–	1	1	2
At least one indoor activity	21	23	25	28
At least one indoor or outdoor activity	N/A	42	44	46

Source: Sports Council (1988)

Interpretation | 6

6.1 INTRODUCTION

Interpretation is considered an essential element of any countryside site; indeed it is one element which sets it apart from a more formal or structured recreational or sports facility. But why interpret, and what is interpretation?

Interpretation has been defined as 'an educational activity which aims to reveal meanings and relationships through the use of original objects, by first hand experience and by illustrative media, rather than simply to communicate factual information' (Tilden, 1967). As such, interpretation is more – much more – than an educational process or a recreational or entertaining experience. Whilst interpretation can be, and often is, all of these things, the integrity of both the quality of information and the means that is employed to communicate the information must remain intact.

To the countryside manager, the 'countryside message' lies at the heart of countryside interpretation. A strict definition of the countryside message is impossible. Key components of it will be: to import an understanding of the various demands upon the countryside; increase the visitor's enjoyment of the site (and the countryside); to transfer information to the visitor; and to help the manager control/manage the resource under his or her control. This process is summarized by Sharpe (1976) as: 'Interpretation seeks to achieve three objectives: the first or primary objective is to assist the visitor in developing a keener awareness, appreciation and understanding of the area he (she) is visiting. The second objective is to accomplish management goals . . . The third objective is to promote public understanding of an agency and its programmes'.

Before we consider the equally important question of 'why interpret?', a final definition of countryside interpretation will give a collective description of the process. The Countryside Commission (1979a) define interpretation as having, as its main concern 'explaining the significance of and encouraging an awareness and understanding of, the landscape and the physical forces which bring about changes and have led to its present appearance'.

The point at which interpretation ceases to be an instructional activity and becomes largely recreational or entertaining is unclear. A private site operator may need to ensure that an interpretive process is entertaining enough for people to want to pay to watch or participate in it. For a publicly owned site or site with a greater degree of natural history importance, the quality of the message may be felt to be more important. However, common to all situations is the requirement that the information can be fully understood by the people for whom it is intended, and that the information is, in itself, of a high factual quality.

Having determined what interpretation actually is, the manager must ask him or herself 'why interpret?' The answer to this question is, in part, given by Sharpe's definition of interpretation given above. However, the question is far broader than this. If, for example, interpretation seeks to meet management objectives there may be more appropriate means of meeting these objectives. Similarly, some sites may be interesting and attractive and thus worthy of interpretation, but may in some way be devalued by, for example, a notice board. Finally, the process of interpretation is not cheap and priorities must always be considered by the manager.

The manager must be prepared to consider, therefore, that a site should not be interpreted for any one of a variety of reasons. Having determined that an interpretation programme for a particular site is required, the manager needs to assess the interpretive process and plan its implementation carefully.

6.2 INTERPRETIVE PLANNING

Figure 6.1 shows a diagrammatic representation of the interpretive planning process. The flow diagram can be summarized as consisting of four key questions: why interpret, what should be interpreted, for whom should it be interpreted, and how should it be interpreted? Interpretive planning can usefully be discussed under these broad headings.

6.2.1 Why interpret?

There are several reasons behind the process of interpretation, some of which have been identified above. Objectives such as: increasing the visitor's enjoyment of a site; increasing understanding; satisfying local demand for information; meeting sponsors' needs; and helping the management process, are all reasons which may, collectively, underlie the decision to interpret a countryside site.

As there is such a diverse group of objectives, the manager must ensure that these objectives are clearly understood and prioritized. As the Countryside Commission (1979a) indicate: 'The precise objective of any interpretive programme should be stated at the outset'. If some confusion arises over the programme objectives, this will manifest itself in confused implementation later in the process.

6.2.2 What can be interpreted?

Having established, first, that interpretation is appropriate and desirable, and secondly why an interpretation programme is to be created, the manager must also assess the characteristics of the site which can be interpreted. Once again, there is a list of types of site features that are worthy of environmental interpretation. Such a list would include: geological/ecological features; archaeological and landscape features, for example, views or literary associations, or heritage/cultural features.

The question 'why' and 'what' are inextricably linked, and one will have a bearing on the other, but all sites have a message or a story that is worth relating. Similarly, however, all sites impose constraints upon the interpretive process, which must also be borne in mind. A remote, semi-natural resource will not be the most sympathetic location for a large notice board, nor indeed the localized pressure that might result from such a feature. The accessibility of the site may also affect what may or may not be interpreted – unexposed rock strata, for example, are not very exciting for most people!

Management constraints too will impose restrictions on the interpretive process. Delicate sites will not respond well to concentration of visitors, and peak demand will pose its own problems in a visitor centre, for example. Furthermore, it is conceivable that an interpretive programme will be at odds with the overall management objective for the site.

In determining what is to be interpreted, therefore, the interplay of the physical, management and human environments needs to be assessed.

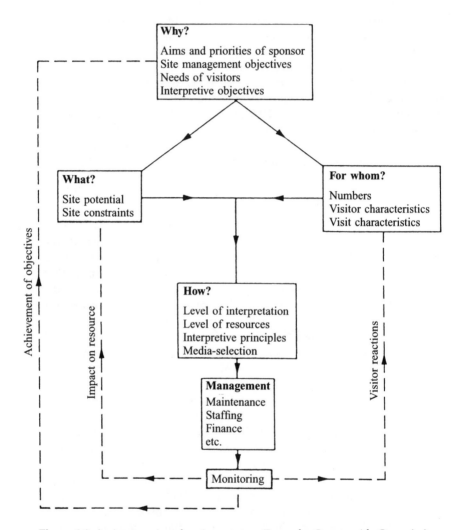

Figure 6.1 An interpretive planning process. From the Countryside Commission (1979a).

6.2.3 For whom?

The manager of any recreation facility must continually ask the question: for whom is the provision being made? This is, therefore, a truism for the provision of interpretation. However, it is necessary to re-emphasize the importance of the question, because it determines the quantity, location, medium, characteristics and distribution of the interpretive programme.

The target audience for the interpretation can form a segment of the overall visitors to the countryside site. Important considerations will be: age, structure of a group, reading or other abilities, length of stay on-

---

1. What scale of use is anticipated?

2. What might be the pattern of visits? Variation in visitor patterns by hours, days or seasons will all have implications for site management.

3. How long might visitors stay? How long does the management want them to stay?

4. What is known of group size and structure? Would visitors be mainly family groups, school parties, etc?

5. Are school parties likely to be so numerous that special facilities would have to be provided for them?

6. What is the likely age structure of visiting groups? What special facilities would be needed for the very young or the very old?

7. What are the socio-economic characteristics of the likely visitors? This knowledge could influence the intellectual level or pricing policy for any facilities provided.

8. Where might visitors come from? Would they be on holiday, day out, education, business? Place of residence or origin could suggest clues for interpretive themes (e.g. historical connections between site and home area). Holiday areas may have a more regular weekly use but greater seasonal fluctuations.

9. Are repeat visits likely? Should they be encouraged and catered for? Repeat visits are most likey in areas of day visitor use. Inflexible (and usually expensive) facilities are less appropriate where there are high levls of repeat visits.

10. Should any special needs of visitors be catered for: e.g. blind or disabled, or non-English speakers?

11. What aspects of the site are particularly likely to interest visitors: e.g. are there any unique or dramatic features on which an interpretive programme might capitalize?

Figure 6.2 How to identify target group for interpretation. From the Countryside Commission (1979a).

site, location of entry/exit on to site, regularity of visit and special needs. The Countryside Commission (1979a) identify 11 sets of criteria and parameters which will require consideration before a manager assembles an interpretive programme (these are given in Figure 6.2).

Marketing the interpretive programme is essential. This entails not only identifying the people for whom the interpretation is intended, but also identifying their needs, and monitoring the process to ensure that the provision and the requirements of the public coincide.

6.2.4 How should we interpret?

This question entails much more than assessing which one of a large number of media is most appropriate. The location of the interpretation on the site is important, as too is the timing of the interpretation. These decisions can, however, only be made when the foregoing analysis has been undertaken. To summarize, the countryside interpretation process must seek to cover the points listed below.

- Interpretation provides more than factual information. It should explain and evoke a response.
- Interpretation should present a complete picture, emphasizing the whole.
- Most people absorb a message if contained within a story.
- To achieve optimum impact, the interpretation should relate to the age, ability, personality of the visitor.
- Visitors must enjoy the interpretation, otherwise they will not relate to the message.
- Visitors will usually enjoy a variety of media, becoming bored if one medium is over used.
- An interpretive programme can be split into several units, each using the most appropriate medium and format.
- Interpretation is a skill in itself which requires expertise and training – knowledge of a subject does not imply the ability to communicate.
- Some sites do not need interpreting.

Aldridge (1975) and Pennyfather (1975) have assessed the process of countryside interpretation in Britain, and have identified some 63 different types of interpretive techniques. Pennyfather (1975) categorizes these techniques into five broad types, and assesses their effectiveness against 18 criteria, including: impact, flexibility, cost, durability, safety, simplicity and appearance. The five broad types of interpretive techniques are outlined below.

1. Personal service: such as guided walks, talks or expert demon-strations.
2. Participatory media: techniques that involve some level of activity or effort from the visitor. This might include identification of species or acclimatization.
3. Live displays: this will cover events such as dramatic plays, or period-costumed guides.
4. Static displays: this group covers a wide range, from notice boards, publications and displays of stuffed animals to museum-type facilities with large, full-sized exhibits.
5. Gadgets: a now somewhat outdated concept, this group will include videos, audiovisual shows and holograms. Arguably, however, the visitors will expect this relatively technically advanced type of display because most people are familiar with, and used to, this level of sophistication.

Each of these techniques or groups of techniques has its own strengths and weaknesses. It is the role of the manager to assess the correct medium in any given circumstances.

6.2.5 Monitoring and management

Once an interpretive programme is in place, the manager must control and monitor the system just as he or she must manage other parts of the countryside site.

Monitoring will cover elements such as the impact of the interpretation on the resource and upon the visitors, the success of the interpretation in meeting objectives (which in turn re-emphasizes the need for clear objec-tives in the first instance) and the financial success of the interpretation. Visitor enjoyment can be monitored in a number of ways; by interview, by observing, or by patterns of visitor activity. Similarly, the impact of the interpretation on the resource will manifest itself through localized erosion, visitor pressure, visual intrusion, and so on. Records of monitor-ing and a process for rectifying problems is necessary.

Managing the interpretive process is a far wider reaching problem for the manager. Once the interpretation programme is in place, the knock-on effects within the countryside site will be felt in a number of areas. Whilst these effects could, and should, be foreseen and planned for, they will still need to be managed efficiently.

Areas within which the interpretive programme will have an impact include: visitor control; peak demand; staffing levels; charging policy;

Figure 6.3 The countryside is one of the best classrooms available.

overtime requirements; repair budgets; emergency procedures; marketing policy; sales outlets; and overall maintenance of the site fabric.

The best way to oversee this integrated process is to develop an interpretive strategy for a site. Westmacott and Worthington (1975) United States National Park Service (1975) and Robinson (1979) all provide examples of countryside interpretive strategies for countryside recreation sites.

More than any other facility provided by the site manager, interpretation is a continuous process. Car-parks, toilets or footpaths are built, used and maintained, but interpretation involves a continuous feedback process with the visitor. If the message inherent within the interpretation is to reach its target audience, or the interpretive programme is to meet its objectives, the quality of the feedback process needs constant supervisions. By concentrating upon this quality, the manager will provide an enjoyable and valuable contribution to managing the countryside and to the people who seek to enjoy its beauty and uniqueness.

6.3 INTERPRETIVE TECHNIQUES

Within the constraints imposed by this text, it is impossible to detail all possible methods of interpretation. As we have seen, Pennyfather (1975) has identified 63 different techniques, each of which will require different considerations and skills from the manager. This chapter covers just six of the more common techniques: leaflets; display boards; guided walks/ talks; self-guide trails; audiovisual displays; and acclimatization. It is worth stressing, however, that although these techniques are common, they should still be exposed to the same scrutiny as other techniques. A leaflet will nearly always be produced for a countryside site, but what is it trying to achieve; for whom is it intended; and would other techniques have a similar impact, or be more efficient? Therefore, whilst the following techniques are given as relatively common, their use and effectiveness need to be monitored and managed none the less.

6.3.1 Leaflets

The preconditions of countryside interpretation given earlier in this chapter hold equally for leaflets and other individual media used for interpretation. What must concern us here, therefore, are the specific advantages and disadvantages that are characteristic of leaflets.

'Leaflets' cover many different types of countryside publication from a relatively scientific specialist booklet to a single flysheet carrying little information at all. Whatever the type of publication, the concept of the leaflet is that it can usually be provided cheaply (if not completely free) to the visitor, it is designed for use off- or on-site and contains varying degrees of information for the visitor.

Vasey (1985) identifies a series of key stages within the process of planning a leaflet or other on-site publication. First, it is necessary to put the publication in context with other interpretive provision on site.

This means not only assessing whether the leaflet is the most appropriate medium, but also coordinating all interpretive provision. A leaflet fulfils a relatively specific role, in that it is a one-way medium; it requires some effort to read but can also be taken home once the visit has ended. The leaflet, therefore, has its strengths and weaknesses.

Having put the leaflet in context, the manager must clearly identify the target audience and the purpose and objectives of the publication. This will then dictate the format and material used for the production and the overall design and content. If the publication is to be used outside, for example, it must be durable but also easy to handle. Similarly a simplified map may help inexperienced map readers, and may encour-

Figure 6.4 One of the most basic requirements is a leaflet giving location, opening times, facilities and other information.

age people to explore sites for themselves. Furthermore, by simply not putting some areas of the site on the map, visitors can be directed away from these areas.

Funding the leaflet may or may not be a problem, but high-quality, full-colour leaflets are expensive. One possible way of offsetting this cost is through sponsorship or advertising. Furthermore, over ambitious print runs may result in misspent money and lost capital.

Having determined the objectives of the leaflets, the actual design and production process may be tackled by the manager's staff, or by outside design experts. Whether or not the manager actually employs graphic or other design staff will depend on the amount of such work generated by the site. Working with design staff as with any specialists, requires mutual cooperation and understanding. The manager must be prepared to give the designer a full brief, which gives details of all of the relevant considerations. The manager must then work closely through the stages of production.

Finally, having printed the leaflet, the manager must consider the outlets for publication, and must ensure that stocks are kept at these outlets. Also, the manager must monitor the success or otherwise of the leaflet: through questionnaires; observation; or whatever means are appropriate. There is little doubt that a well-planned leaflet is an asset to a countryside site, but the manager must ensure that, as with everything else, the leaflet is well thought out, well researched and well produced.

6.3.2 Display boards

Display boards, either internally or externally located, can be defined as boards that have an interpretive rather than a simply directional or instructural message. As such, boards are usually located at key circulation points, such as entrances, forks in roads or footpaths or at visitor centres. There are several materials used to produce display boards. Figure 6.5 shows the percentage of use made of some of the commoner materials (from a survey sample of Local Authorities and charitable trusts). Lindesay (1985) has categorized these materials on the basis of their cost, durability, ease of maintenance and availability. Needless to say, each material and type of board has its own characteristic advantages and disadvantages.

The process of planning, scripting and siting display boards has several key stages (Piersenne, 1985). The aim of the display panel, as with other methods of interpretation, is to encourage and interest the visitor and provide him or her with information about the site, and its history or natural history.

The key points for display boards can be summarized. First, question not just the appropriateness of interpretation, but also the suitability of a display board in particular. A particularly valuable, semi-natural landscape or an historic building may not be appropriate sites for permanent display panels. As well as the physical appropriateness a site may be best interpreted through another medium because of cultural or other constraints. This process of decision making precedes all elements of interpretation.

Having decided that a display board is the most appropriate medium, its location, size, mounting and design must be considered. In order to place these stages in context, we must decide why a panel is most appropriate in some circumstances. A display board gives on-site information at the exact location at which the manager knows the information is required. Therefore, panels should be located to relate to the objects to which they refer, but should not be obtrusive so as

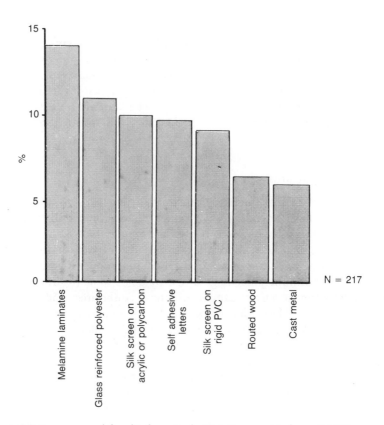

Figure 6.5 Systems used for display panels (%). Source: Lindesay (1985).

to detract from the scene that is being interpreted. Similarly, the size, shape, material and general ambience of the panel should fit into the surrounding environment. A simple but exemplary case of this can be seen with the panels used by the National Trust, which are made from routed wood (see Figure 6.6).

The internal design of the board will not only relate to the surrounding environment, but also the target audience, and other practical considerations such as how close to the board readers will be able to stand, and how the information is to be given – through words, photographs, line drawings or illustrations or a combination of these elements. It is inevitable that casual observers will respond to panels differently from dedi-

Figure 6.6 Good display and information boards are crucial to effective on-site interpretation and visitor management.

cated experts and will, therefore, require different media and levels of information.

Thus, the actual information content will need to be gauged carefully. Too much information will confuse some visitors, too little will not supply the requirements of the visitors. Piersenne (1985) defines this situation by pointing out 'You can't possibly say everything: so be firm and select priorities. The content must be relevant and don't be too clever!'

One good method of overcoming the problem of a technicality in text or layout is to have a non-technical member of staff review it or, better still, have a pilot run on members of the target audience. If this is done at the draft or 'mock-up' stage, alterations will not be too costly and will make the overall design more effective.

6.3.3 Guided walks

The guided walk is still one of the best ways of communicating information and introducing members of the public to the opportunities and beauty to be found in the natural environment. Nothing rubs off like enthusiasm, and countryside staff are nothing if not enthusiastic!! However, the guided walk is a medium for interpretation and must, therefore, be viewed alongside other media, and on its merits. The Countryside Commission (1980c) identify the pitfalls of relying upon the guided walk and a programme of guided walks to achieve too much. For example, guided walkers are already predisposed to visit a countryside site. The walks do not, in themselves, necessarily attract people who might not otherwise visit the countryside. As the Countryside Commission (1980c) suggest 'Demand cannot be stimulated simply by ensuring that the maximum number of people are made aware of the existence of the programme'.

There is a major distinction to be drawn between the individual guided walks and the programme of guided walks. In the former, the content is of importance, and in the latter, the overall package of a series of events is important.

A programme of guided walks may be felt appropriate to provide a series of points of view about a particular site, or to reach a wide audience, each walk attracting a different target audience. People may attend a particular subject-based walk, and not attend others. Some evidence does exist that visitors to countryside sites may enjoy a guided walk almost irrespective of the subject. Thus, the objectives of a programme of guided walks must be weighed against what such a programme can realistically achieve.

For guided walks to be accessible, the timing, start/finish points, and terrain over which they go must be carefully considered to match target groups. And all of this comes before the actual content of the walk is planned. Indeed, it is perhaps more useful to start the planning of a guided walks programme from each individual walk. 'Walks should only be organized to meet demand' (Countryside Commission, 1980c). A walk should be planned to match people with a particular place, and strike a balance and understanding between the two elements. A guided walk will, therefore, be appropriate in circumstances where a site is known to be popular, and where a demand is known to exist for information, but where on-site or leaflet provision, for example, is not appropriate. The people best placed to measure this demand will usually be site rangers who, most likely, will also lead the guided walk.

Under these circumstances, a guided walk will be an effective medium for interpretation. Thus, the emphasis must be on walk content, not a programme package. It is conceivable that individual walks may add up to a programme, but this is not necessarily the case. For example, a guided walk may be just one element of a more entertainment-based series of on-site activities, such as events, craft fairs or displays. The guided walk *per se* appeals to a very specific market, but within that context is an effective method of communication. This restricted market indicates that advertising, walk content and other administrative consideration can be equally targeted.

6.3.4 Self-guided trails

By contrast to guided walks, a self-guided trail relies heavily upon the visitor taking responsibility for locating, following and understanding the trail which has been provided by the manager. Their history in Britain is one of the longest of any interpretive medium commonly used in the countryside. As Dyke (1986) states 'The self-guide trail was the first interpretive medium to be introduced on a large scale in the development of the countryside interpretation in Britain in the early 1960s. It was first used in the form of nature trails, then in forest interpretation and more recently as one of the means of interpreting farming, ancient monuments and towns'.

At its simplest level, a self-guided trail can be a circular walk that takes people around a site and seeks to stimulate interest through closer contact with the environment. At its most sophisticated, a self-guided trail may entail a variety of routes, with audio equipment or interpretive panels along the route, and possibly printed back-up material. The constraints that govern the type of provision are those that govern all interpretive decisions, namely: management objectives; project objectives; funding; target audience; physical constraints; and resources required for management/maintenance.

Having established management and project objectives, and determined target groups, the manager must create the trail through a logical series of steps. These are: survey; design; implementation; interpretation; maintenance and promotion (Wilkinson, 1985).

Survey Because a self-guide trail is a physical entity, in order to establish a valuable, interesting and (just as importantly) safe route, a survey must be undertaken to identify the optimum route or routes for a site trail. This should take account of the nature of the environment and the types of people who will be expected to use the trail. Physically disabled and blind people will clearly require different conditions from school children, for example, although a range of groups need not necessarily be mutually exclusive.

If the trail is to be based upon public-rights-of-way, it is necessary to have an understanding of the legal considerations of the rights-of-way system (Clayden and Trevelyan, 1983).

Design The level of required design will vary with the natural environment and the target audience. Practical consideration of path design will always be important (surface material, drainage problems and so on) and these can be handled confidently by landscape designers or others with suitable experience or training (British Trust for Conservation Volunteers, 1983). Less obvious consideration may include additional planting to increase interest, tapping rails for blind people, viewing points and more obviously, consideration for waymarking and on-site directions.

Implementation Implementation may include no more than adequately sign posting an existing path or series of paths. Slightly more developed than this would be the installation of new or better path furniture (gates to allow wheelchair access, stiles or fencing). At the other extreme, whole new path systems may have to be created, with electrical supplies laid on for audio-equipment or listening posts. There will inevitably be a need, within all of these types of provisions, for a consistency in design and implementation to give the trail a unique and identifiable 'feel'. Information panels or waymarks will, therefore, need to be readily identifiable as belonging to the particular route.

Interpretation The medium actually used on the trail can vary, despite the fact that the trail itself can be considered as a medium. On-site information boards will provide easily accessible information, but may prove intrusive. Numbered posts can give easy reference to an accompanying leaflet but give no information to people without leaflets. As with all elements of countryside management, the manager must be clear from the outset what is to be interpreted and for whom it is to be interpreted. This will give a good indication of the type of interpretation to be used, in this case, on the self-guided trail.

Maintenance A specially promoted trail should not suffer from neglect. It does not take a lot to discourage many visitors to the countryside from venturing or exploring and thus understanding. A blocked or overgrown path is such a discouragement which, on the public-right-of-way system as a whole, is a very common feature (Countryside Commission, 1989). The resources available to manage the trail must, therefore, be taken into consideration when devising the facility.

Promotion Promoting a self-guided trail ensures not only that the route is used, but also gives the trail an 'image' which will help visitors to understand its relevance and its basic message.

Thus, phrases like Nature Trail, Woodland Walk, Heritage Trail and Valley Way will help to provide the manager and the visitor with a useful concept with which to promote and interpret a self-guided trail.

6.3.5 Audiovisual techniques

Audiovisual interpretation in itself covers a wide range of individual techniques from the manually generated slide show/talk to an entirely automated, hologram and laser show! However, the internal definition of interpretation must still be maintained. If the medium does not interpret the countryside, for our purposes it cannot be considered as interpretation, however entertaining and high tech.

Research suggests that the senses of sight and hearing collectively absorb some 80–90% of all stimuli. An audiovisual presentation, therefore, stands a large chance of at least being seen and/or heard by the visitor; this is the first crucial stage in ensuring that a message meets its objectives.

The Countryside Commission (1980c) identifies two types of situations within which audiovisual techniques are appropriate: where their use is optimal given all constraints such as staff availability, cost or buildings; and when dealing with the uncommitted visitor and gaining attention is important.

As we have seen, there is a wide variety of audiovisual media, and the mechanical techniques are just one group. It is clear that the advantages of such a system need to be weighed up before the high capital outlay on these techniques is made. The advantages that audiovisual techniques have can be summarized as follows:

- They present information through media that are readily understood by most people;
- They can show a condensed time sequence and before and after shots;
- They are always available.
- They can operate without attendant staff if necessary and are pre-planned;
- Audiovisual techniques can provide a consistently high standard of performance.

Audiovisual presentations do have some disadvantages, such as the increased level of sophistication which involves greater levels of necessary technical skill, and the need for a specialist environment, such as a building or room. The disadvantages as such are mainly a result of comparing audiovisual media with other techniques – the direct contact with a ranger, or the unexpected nature of a self-guide trail suggest that other media are appropriate in many situations. However, carefully managed, the audiovisual media are a popular and potentially powerful means of interpreting a site; a means which requires a high degree of specialist knowledge, even at a very basic level (Kodak, 1976; Overman, 1977).

6.3.6 Acclimatization

The final interpretive medium to be discussed is that of acclimatization. It is unique from the other media discussed previously because it is more an approach to interpretation rather than an individual technique. Acclimatization was first formulated by Van Matre (1972) in the USA, where many of Britain's models for countryside recreational provision originate. Since its conception, it has become one of the strongest components of modern countryside interpretation. It is based upon the principles of total sensory immersion in the natural environment, and attempting to view that environment through different perspectives. It is simply not enough to touch or hear or see in a shallow way, but the objective of acclimatization is to try to regain, however briefly, some of the lost sense of contact and partnership with the natural environment.

To reach such a depth of awareness, acclimatization has several characteristics. First, a great deal of time clearly has to be spent with each visitor to involve them in such a programme. Thus, it is of little value to one-off or occasional visitors. Secondly, it involves a great degree of commitment from the participants; this occasionally involves visitors exploring their own emotions as much as the nature of their surroundings. Thirdly, the approach can only work if personal guidance is used – written explanations of how to imagine yourself as a hedgehog or a tree are difficult to perceive! Thus, acclimatization is about awakening awareness and removing modern obstacles to learning.

As a concept for most situations, therefore, it is of limited use. But where a manager can attract return visitors who would value such an input, it is a valuable and exciting approach to interpretation. Particularly relevant groups might include school parties, existing committed environmental groups and, indeed, other countryside staff, including the manager. After all we all have something to learn from the natural environment.

6.4 SUMMARY

There can be several aims to an interpretive programme. Hence, the first priority of the manager is to set the objectives for this element of his or her overall provision. As elsewhere, clear objectives are vital, and this is particularly the case for interpretation programmes, because interpretation represents a characteristic of countryside site management: an appropriate level of interpretation is integral to recreation site management.

The public's appetite for information on the natural environment seems insatiable, and it is the responsibility of the manager to provide this information when and where it will be valuable and through a medium that will be easily and readily understood by the target audience.

As Bishop Creighton said in the late 19th century: 'The one real objective of education, is to leave a man so that he is continually asking questions'.

Marketing | 7

7.1 INTRODUCTION

The concept of marketing the natural environment is still a relatively
new one. None the less, it is now well accepted that many of the
principles of marketing can be applied to the countryside and the recreational opportunities available within it. The manager must, however,
be clear about the role that he or she wants marketing to play within
the overall site management, otherwise it is unlikely to succeed.

The difficulty in accepting marketing as a mechanism for assisting
the manager is likely to arise as a result of a misunderstanding of the
principles of marketing rather than anything fundamentally wrong with
marketing as a concept.

The aim of marketing is to 'try to ensure that the requirements of
people or organizations are continuously matched by opportunities and
resources' (Clay, 1984). This is a concept which is a long way removed
from the image of hard sell or product-orientated, foot-in-the-door
advertising. The process of establishing people's requirements of the
countryside, assessing the potential and constraints of a site and trying
to match the countryside site with visitors' requirements is an inevitable
consequence of providing a countryside recreation site: recreation implies
that people have certain requirements that need to be met. At its simplest
level many people require 'peace and quiet' or 'somewhere natural'.
Meeting these visitor requirements should not conflict with the natural
history and landscape objectives of a countryside recreation site manager.
(This would, however, be a different situation on a nature reserve or
extremely delicate habitat.)

More detailed or sophisticated provision is more difficult to assess,
but still necessary. However, Torkildsen (1986) suggests that it is not
unknown for some providers of recreational resources to provide facili-

ties, buildings, events, programmes, opening times and other opportunities without reference to the eventual users.

The process of marketing redresses this imbalance by providing a framework for the views of users to influence decisions made by the manager. Kotler (1975) has assessed the relevance of the marketing process to non-profit-based organizations and concludes that the process can be applied equally to profit-based private enterprise and non-profit based Local Authorities and charitable trusts.

More specifically, the leisure or recreational provision can be marketed equally in the profit- or non-profit-based organizations and management. Craig (1989) has emphasized the importance of marketing for the public sector where 'other objectives' such as social and economic equality, and access for deprived groups may be equally as important as increasing income levels. For countryside recreation site managers, these other considerations will clearly include the integrity of the natural environment, the visual amenity of the area and the physical constraints of the site.

If we, therefore, accept that a working definition of marketing is to try to ensure that the requirements of people or organizations are continually met by opportunities and resources, this leads on to further analysis.

Clearly, the term 'people' does not cover every single individual; their needs are not all identical. School children, single parents, elderly couples or disabled people will all require different things from the same or different sites. The overall market needs to be divided into a number of subgroups: market segments. Market segmentation can be undertaken on a variety of criteria, the commonest being age, sex and socio-economic status. Across these broad bands, however, other criteria could further subdivide the community. The process of defining market segmentation is in itself complex but a necessary prerequisite of determining visitor needs.

The working definition being used here further suggests that marketing is a continuous process, as indeed it should be. Existing user groups need to be reviewed against management targets. The views of these groups and individuals should be assessed and changes (if necessary) need to be made to the site; new footpaths, fewer man-made intrusions, more guided walks, and so on. This implies that the product (the site of the opportunities and resources of the above definition) is a multifaceted concept. To different people, a countryside recreation site provides very different opportunities. The role of the manager on a recreation site is to ensure that the facilities provided on the site match the requirements of the numerous market segments. Furthermore, these facilities also have to link into each other and fit sympathetically into the natural environments. The manager is at the pivot of this balancing act.

It is clear that in order to meet visitors' needs, the manager may have to adjust the countryside site, within natural and managerial constraints. There are four elements of the site which can be changed or managed differently, namely, the product, the place, the price and the promotion of the site. Collectively, these are known as the marketing mix; and the balance of the elements of the marketing mix represents the practical application of marketing and management.

7.2 THE MARKETING MIX

The marketing mix represents the adjustments that are made to, in this case, a countryside site in order to try to meet the visitors' requirements and expectations for that site. It must be stressed that the marketing process will be controlled by the manager and should not be seen as a means of 'selling the countryside'; a tactic that would ultimately lead to a decrease in the attractiveness and ecological quality of the countryside. Marketing represents one mechanism for balancing the requirements of the environment, the needs of the manager and the expectations of the visitors.

7.2.1 The product

It may be difficult to view the countryside simply as 'a product'. A can of beans or a car can be seen more easily as a product, but this perception is not so readily accepted for the countryside or the environment. However, if we define a product as no more than the service article or experience that people seek, the countryside does fit this definition of a product.

The facility that the manager offers can be varied as a whole or elements within it can be changed. A countryside recreation site can be un-developed to provide a 'wilderness experience' or, alternatively, it can provide an intensive, semi-formal experience; in a country park, for example. The type of site will depend upon not only the environmental constraints, but also the views of the visitors. There is inevitably a certain amount of circularity in assessing on-site visitor requirements: presumably visitors go to a site because they like the site and, consequently, may not wish to see too many changes. However, visitor surveys are the best way of establishing, first, the requirements of the visitors and secondly, whether on-site provision matches these requirements.

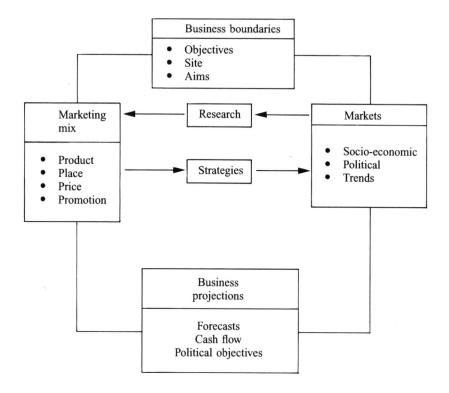

Figure 7.1 The marketing system.

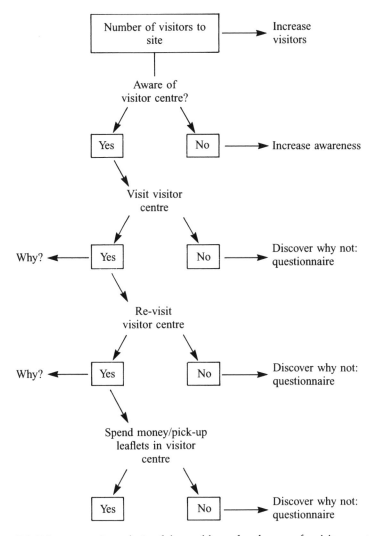

Figure 7.2 Diagrammatic analysis of the problem of under-use of a visitor centre.

There is a large amount of skill required in conducting visitor surveys. The Tourism and Recreation Research Unit (1983) prepared guidelines for conducting visitor surveys. Nottinghamshire County Council (1983) gives a detailed analysis of one such survey, extracts of which are given in Table 7.1. The informality of the two sites, and the relative importance of children in people's plans give some indication of the product that people will be seeking. (Although, without analysing all of the data, such an over simplification could be foolhardy!)

The commonest way of changing the product is to introduce new or different facilities, such as toilets, picnic tables, litter bins, countryside walks or shops. On some sites these will be inappropriate, but for most sites that actively seek to encourage visitors, these facilities will be valuable. Any such addition or indeed, reduction, to the site can be seen as changing the product. These changes must be undertaken in response to visitor needs. The first task for a manager is, therefore, to establish what products or range of products are being provided. This in turn links back directly to the management plan discussed in Chapter 3. The basic, underlying question which the management plan seeks to answer is 'what are we trying to achieve on this site?'. The manager, in defining the product that his or her site offers, is seeking to answer the question 'what business am I in?'. The answer to this may be 'the leisure industry', 'the conservation movement', or 'social services'. Each of these represents a different product and a different method of marketing will be required. The term 'product' can, therefore, relate to a specific, physical aspect of a site, or to the type of experience or service that the site provides.

Product	What is being provided? Why do people use the site/ area? What do they want from the site? What are the 'themes'?
Place	Where is the site? Where are elements of it located?
Price	How much does it cost? Is everything charged separately? What are the financial objectives?
Promotion	What message is required? How is the product to be advertised? What methods are available?

The answers to these and all of the many other questions will be different from site to site, and between marketing segments for each site.

Figure 7.3 The marketing mix.

Table 7.1 Reasons given for visiting two country parks

Base: summer visitors	Total	Park A		Total	Park B	
		First visit	Repeat visit		First visit	Repeat visit
	212 (%)	64 (%)	148 (%)	205 (%)	70 (%)	135 (%)
For a walk/outing in general A day out, e.g. to have a look around or a picnic	29	19	33	36	34	36
To show to friends/relatives, e.g. 'we had visitors staying and wanted to show them the park'	14	8	17	15	11	16
Because of the local interest or historical interest	18	30	14	–	–	–
Passing through or staying in the area, or on holiday in the area at present	10	23	5	10	17	7
To bring the children (any mention of benefits for children)	8	8	8	5	3	7
To visit the craft centre/visitor centre	–	–	–	9	11	8
Convenient to reach. Nearby. Nice distance.	2	3	2	5	3	7
Because of the weather	3	2	3	2	4	1
To buy something	2	–	3	2	–	2
To visit a particular exhibition/event	1	–	2	3	3	3
Off work/not working today	–	–	–	2	6	–
'Just like it in general'	3	–	4	2	1	2
Other	8	6	9	4	1	5
Don't know/no real reason	–	–	–	2	3	1

7.2.2 The place

A countryside recreation site is, often as not, fixed in its location before any attempts are made to manage or market the site. Even a cursory glance at the circumstances surrounding such sites will reveal why this is the case. First, by definition countryside sites need to be in the countryside and whilst this is open to flexible definition, the limits of what is and is not countryside can only be stretched so far. Secondly, the countryside needs to be attractive (although this is in itself, a relative term) so that it will encourage people to visit. Finally, due largely to the economics of land values, it is relatively difficult to establish a new countryside site when in most circumstances new housing or industrial units would be more profitable.

In short, therefore, the location of a countryside recreation site is relatively fixed, unlike that of a sports centre or a museum for example. This does not mean, however, that locational decisions cannot be made by the manager. Broadly speaking, two types of locational options are open to the site manager. First, individual elements of the site can be located in any number of different ways within the site, and these locations can be amended to conform to the desires of the visitors. Some of these locational decisions will not need too much research (toilets near to the car-park, or the visitor centre being located at the entrance to the site, for example). However, other decisions will need to be made in the context of additional information.

The second type of locational change that a manager can make is within the public's perception of site locations. A site that is situated a long way from centres of population (and thus potential visitors) can partly overcome this potential problem by identifying the concerns of the public and providing information that addresses these concerns. Once on site, visitors' perceptions of location and distance can similarly be addressed through site plans, written information or talks, for example. Thus the manager has the opportunity to influence the potential and actual visitors' perceptions of location. This may be particularly important in areas where public transport is weak, or where the site is outside the normal travel patterns of its potential visitors (Henry, 1983). Indeed, this perceptive problem of place is one of the major barriers to participation in any recreational activity, including countryside recreation.

Figure 7.4 The first rule of marketing – let people know you are there!

7.2.3 The price

How much to charge and when and where to charge it is one of the most critical decisions that a manager will make, but taken in isolation from the other elements of a marketing strategy, the decisions about pricing are likely to be misdirected.

Pricing policies will be developed as a result of a large number of influences. The ownership structure of the site for example will determine some of the pricing mechanisms; a Local Authority may wish only to rely upon the funds generated through local government sources or grant aid, whilst a privately managed site may only have site-based charges upon which to rely for income.

A further influence upon pricing policy will clearly be the manager's target markets. A countryside site that seeks to cater largely for school groups or educational needs will have to establish a different pricing framework to a site that targets family or adult groups.

Finally, the pricing policies of nearby, competitive sites will influence the manager's decision. Two identical facilities which have radically different pricing policies will attract different people and different numbers. In setting prices, therefore, the manager needs to establish other prices and what, if anything, he or she is providing that is different from these other sites. It is for this reason that pricing cannot be viewed in isolation from all of the other considerations.

Having established an overall framework for the pricing policy, there are still many decisions to be made. The most immediate is how to charge visitors. Alternatives include a one-off payment for all facilities; a facility-based charge, paid only when each separate facility is used; or a combination/variation of these. Similarly, the manager will have to decide whether some groups will need concessionary charges, and whether income generated from sales should be included within the pricing process. Each of these decisions will have implications on other aspects of the development of the site and, therefore, requires careful consideration (Vaughan, 1988).

7.2.4 Promotion

The promotional aspects of marketing are often all that is readily noticeable of the process. It is clear, however, that promoting a site comes at the end of a longer and more detailed series of activities that seeks to ensure that the site is designed and managed in a way that matches the expectations of visitors and of management. The promotional work, therefore, aims at informing visitors and potential visitors that not only does the site exist, but that it also provides a series of attractions and opportunities. This may involve no more than developing a leaflet (designed to appeal to the target market) identifying what is available or the services on offer. Alternatively promotion may involve a multidirectional series of events, each aimed at different target markets, and promoting different elements of the site, and using varied but none the less appropriate media. Most countryside recreation sites will, however, err on the side of the former rather than the latter. As long as this meets the marketing objectives, this is all that may be required.

The key concept in developing promotional material, as with all other elements of marketing, is to determine what the site offers the visitor, not what the manager thinks he or she is providing. This will influence not only the methods used, but also the terminology used and the image created to promote the site. Thus, visitor centres may become 'The Ravens Nest', a public footpath may be named 'The Wilderness Way' and public transport routes to countryside sites may become 'The Countryside Explorer'.

The degree to which these promotional techniques are adopted for each site will, ultimately, be decided upon by the manager and his or her employers. It is worth stressing that the marketing process has to be managed, and does not dictate to the manager what should or should not happen on a particular site. That decision always lies with the manager.

7.2.5 Summary

The marketing mix is simply a tool to help the manager assess how changes can be made to the facility that he or she operates. This does not imply that change has to be made, or that changes have to be dramatic. However, to ignore the notion that change should be at least considered is to ignore the prerequisite that a countryside recreation site exists to offer a service and a recreational opportunity to visitors. Other objectives and constraints will clearly operate and these can be accommodated within the management plan.

There still exists in the minds of many countryside managers the belief that the countryside cannot be marketed or that marketing concepts somehow devalue the natural environment. However, whether or not the manager is marketing a commercial operation, he or she will be marketing anyway. The question then becomes whether he or she is controlling the marketing process well or poorly. Good marketing can accommodate not only the more easily recognized commercial considerations, but also political, social and community as well as environmental objectives.

7.3 MARKETING STRATEGY

It will come as no surprise that the only way to assimilate all of the necessary information and create the optional programme of work is to prepare a marketing strategy. Torkildsen (1986) identifies eight stages to this process.

1. Define what is to be achieved: the objective could be designing and opening a new visitor centre or developing a ranger service, or simply informing the target groups of existing facilities.
2. Collect relevant information: this information needs to provide very specific detail, such as what is the nature of the 'product', who will use it, what is the competition to the product, how do people perceive the product and so on. Other characteristic circumstances also need

to be considered at this stage, such as political constraints or social objectives.

3. Set objectives: this part of the strategic planning process involves setting identifiable and measurable targets, related directly to the marketing process. Examples might include raising the level of visitor awareness of a particular facility, or increasing the number of visitors to a site.

4. Establish the course of action: this is the programming stage of the strategy, and will involve establishing who will implement specific parts of the strategy. It is at this stage that adjustments to the marketing mix will actually be identified. Clearly, this stage also requires close coordination and cooperation of staff within the organization.

5. Put the plan down in writing: having agreed with all the necessary individuals the details of the plan, it should be written down. This will at least allow it to be monitored more effectively.

6. Implement the plan: coordinating the programme and overseeing its implementation is the job of the site manager. Changes to the marketing mix must be under the control of the manager, having been agreed in the overall planning process.

7. Monitoring: a critical but often neglected stage of any planning exercise is that of monitoring. This will start with measuring out-turns against the marketing objectives – are the visitor numbers up on last year, or has the quality of the educational service increased? This in turn may necessitate going back to the visitors to obtain more back-up information.

8. Modify the strategy: if the objectives are not being met, the strategy will need to be amended. If they are being met all well and good, but the manager must keep monitoring the process.

7.4 MARKETING IN ACTION

In many industries, marketing is a multimillion pound process, which is correspondingly complex. For many countryside sites this will not necessarily be the case, although the leisure industry is becoming increasingly all embracing, and if we accept that countryside recreation sites are part of the leisure industry, marketing could become equally labyrinthine. However, many problems which face managers are relatively localized and can be resolved by local application of marketing techniques. This case study provides an example of one such situation.

Many country parks or countryside estates have, as part of their operation, a visitor centre. As we saw in Chapter 5, a visitor centre can be any one of, or combination of, a range of facilities, from a toilet block to a restaurant and book shop. In truth, it will invariably fulfil several functions for various groups. Managers of countryside recreation sites are obviously keen for as many visitors as possible to actually use the centre; not only does this allow the manager the opportunity to introduce the countryside, manage, and inform the visitor of other facilities on-site, but it also gives the visitor a chance to sit, use the toilets, buy leaflets or eat. Thus, the centre provides a valuable service for both visitor and manager alike.

It is important, therefore, that where a visitor centre is provided on-site, a large proportion of visitors use such a centre so that they and the manager can benefit from that use. Marketing techniques can be applied to assess why, in certain circumstances, visitor numbers are not as high as expected. This concern over visitor numbers may be triggered by any number of monitoring processes used by management – questionnaire surveys, financial targets or observation, for example. In order to overcome the problem of low visitor numbers the marketing strategy can, as defined earlier, be implemented. Figure 7.2 shows a diagrammatic representation of how this process might operate within this specific circumstance.

The first task is to clearly establish visitor numbers to the recreation site, and to establish what proportion of visitors use the centre. Any number of influences may affect the use/non-use ratio, such as how and through which site entrance visitors arrive, the size of the party, whether children are members of the group and so on. Obviously one of the most important factors is whether or not visitors are aware of the centre, and this can only be determined through questionnaire work. Even if visitors are aware of the centre, they may or may not use it, or having used it once they may or may not re-visit the centre. Again, this can be as a result of any one of a number of reasons: visitors may not be aware of what the centre has to offer, may not feel that it offers anything appropriate to their needs, may be disappointed with what they find, or may simply want to stay away from busy areas within the site. Reasons for non-use need to be determined at this point. Finally, although a proportion of visitors to the site will actually use the centre, the update of leaflets/information or spending on merchandise may be disproportionately lower. This again needs resolving with the views of the customers and visitors being compared with those of the manager and with the services on offer.

Action could be taken at any one of the separate points within this process, but what matters to the manager is taking the course of action that is most effective and that, usually, does not incur the greatest cost

Figure 7.5 In order to develop 'the product' new and innovative techniques may be needed. But the manager needs to be sure the site will not suffer.

in terms of money and effort. Simply raising the overall visitor numbers may, in turn, raise the number of people who visit the centre. However, the ratio of use/non-use will more than likely remain the same. A more effective means of raising levels of use might be to raise overall levels of awareness about the centre, and just as importantly what it has to offer. Its attractions can be understood by asking or observing visitors to the centre, for it can be suggested that if one target group of visitors finds the centre useful and interesting; so too will other members of that group.

This introduces one of the more fundamental principles of marketing: namely that it is easier to raise levels of use amongst existing target groups (either by introducing new members of the same group, or by encouraging re-visits) than it is to stimulate new target areas. In many circumstances, this may not be a problem, but for Local Authorities, for example, it may be politically critical that new target groups are reached; the disabled, single-parent groups or disadvantaged children, for

example. Similarly, for county wildlife trusts where financial viability relies heavily upon levels of membership, it may be a matter of the utmost importance that new target groups are encouraged to join the trust. In order that these new target groups can be encouraged, the trust would have to establish what it could offer these groups and whether this matched the groups' expectations.

This is a relatively simple example of how the marketing concept can be brought to bear on a management problem. This problem could be financial, social, political or a combination of these; what is important is that the views, attitudes and concerns of the visitors or potential visitors are an integral part of the management process. Marketing offers a means of ensuring that this is the case.

Creswell Heritage Trust is a small, independent charity which manages, amongst other sites, a scheduled Ancient Monument at Creswell Crags. The Trust undertook a market survey of existing users, and its catchment profile within 1 hours drive. The product that the Trust wanted to promote was not just a pleasant day out (in this it needed to compete with larger sites close by) but also the educational product of the site which would enable people to learn about the site and its importance for prehistoric records, archaeology, natural history and its records of climatic change found in undisturbed cave deposits stretching back over 150 000 years.

Target figures of 100 000 visits per annum were set, as too were target markets for the various themes, and target incomes. Advertising, merchandising information/interpretation and pricing policies were set against these targets. A five year plan was drawn up, with half yearly reports/monitoring going back to the Board of Trustees.

By developing such a strategy, the Trust could not only safeguard its valuable cave resource, but also meet its charitable objectives and reach realistic financial and educational objectives as well.

Whilst the Trust was only a small operation, the principles of marketing and sound follow-up management were followed. 'A small thing done well.'

Figure 7.6 Marketing: a case study.

7.5 SUMMARY

In 1984 at the Countryside Recreation Research Advisory Group Conference it was suggested (Robinson, 1984) that 'what is of most importance is that countryside recreation management is primarily recreation management, not countryside management'. Robinson then went on to identify the style of management that this re-alignment of views required. Included within this was the role that marketing played '. . . people are clinging to their specialism and failing to recognise that the actual need

should be centred on the user' (Robinson, 1984). For these views, the speaker was subjected to some criticism about the problems that this might bring to the resource under the manager's control. It is clear, however, that the decision as to how far the resource can or should be adapted to meet the requirements of the users will be with the manager. Thus, 'Marketing is matching the users actual or prospective needs to the ability of the resources under the managers to guide demand so that it can produce more, less or different users, or more users from one place to another . . . it should be used to manage demand so that the countryside resource is protected' (Robinson, 1984). This indicates clearly that there is no inherent conflict between the objectives of marketing and those of protecting the countryside for its intrinsic and its recreational importance. The crucial factors are the ability of the environment to support the demands and potential demands of the visitor and, of equal importance, the professional judgement of the manager in balancing the numerous pressures on the site.

The legal framework | 8

8.1 INTRODUCTION

The British legal system is complex, and nowhere is this complexity more obvious than in the issue of land use. An already intricate system of land and land-use law in England and Wales is further complicated by the fact that both Scotland and Northern Ireland have separate legal systems operating within them. This chapter can, therefore, offer no more than a framework for the manager by identifying the main issues that must be addressed by anyone who manages land and by people who specifically manage land for informal recreational purposes.

The British legal system is based upon two sources of legislation: one which is laid down as statute, usually by Parliament; and case law built up from principles developed in the courts.

8.1.1 Statute

Most Acts of Parliament are initiated by the Government of the day. These can be applied to the whole of the United Kingdom, but more often than not separate legislation is enacted for Scotland and Northern Ireland. Hence, the Countryside Act (1968) for England and Wales was mirrored by the Countryside (Scotland) Act. One of the outcomes of this was to establish separate Countryside Commissions for England/Wales and Scotland. The ultimate legal authority in the United Kingdom is Parliament although some powers for appeal or formation of legislation are increasingly being transferred to the European Community.

8.1.2 Case law

Case law consists of the body of decisions made by judges in the high courts. Again, England and Wales share a common court system, and

Scotland and Northern Ireland have separate systems. The reason for this is historical: the case law process is based upon systems of law developed from local customs, feudal systems or tradition. For the managers of land, it is clear that the judiciary's attitude towards matters such as the amenity value of land, the sanctity of private ownership over public concern or the cultural importance and value of land are important. Many of the commoner legal considerations arise out of case law or civil proceedings: nuisance, negligence and trespass, for example.

Increasingly, single issues can give rise to both criminal and civil proceedings and both of these can run consecutively. A land owner who develops a facility without the necessary permissions would be liable to civil proceedings from their neighbours. Furthermore, if the development had taken place through a contract between the manager, and a contractor, the various parties would undoubtedly lead to liability in law for breach of contract. This complexity has led Harte (1985) to suggest 'Legal categories overlap and need to be treated with caution. The law has been likened to a seamless garment. Many of the classifications used to divide up the law so that it can be studied in a manageable form result from its historical development . . . it is now thoroughly entwined'.

However complex the system, it is true without question that land ownership and land use issues are of utmost concern to the British legal system. This reflects the British belief in the right of land ownership. This is indicated by the fact that any agreement which involves a land transaction must be written as a legally binding contract; despite common belief, some contracts can be entered into verbally or through the actions of various parties, but for land, agreements can be made only in writing.

8.2 STATUTORY LAW

Statutory controls for land use clearly have a major impact upon countryside recreation sites. The development of the land, the use made of the land and the safety of people on the land are all issues that are covered by statute which is in turn elaborated upon by the history of cases. A piece of written legislation is inevitably open to interpretation, and as test cases appear, these definitions need to be explored by the legal profession. Thus, for example, the 1968 Countryside Act states that 'In the exercise of their functions relating to land under any enactment, every Minister, government department and public body shall have regard to the desirability of conserving the natural beauty and amenity of the countryside' (Department of the Environment, 1968).

Such a vague concept is clearly open to debate and this debate will usually take the form of test cases within the judicial system.

Notwithstanding the dangers of categorizing legal matters, the statutory framework that most concerns the manager of countryside sites covers three main areas: control of land use; conservation of the natural history and landscape; and the responsibilities of the landowner or occupier of the land.

8.2.1 Land use controls

The planning system of Britain has largely been developed since the end of the Second World War. As part of the physical and social re-building process that took place after 1945, the Town and Country Planning System began to be assembled. Several introductions to this system exist, including Cullingworth (1970), Heap (1973) and Hall (1975). The objective of the planning system is to control and direct the process of development so as to avoid random and directionless activity.

As 'development' had historically been perceived as synonymous with building or industrial activity, most planning legislation relates to these types of activity, with the more 'traditional' rural activities of farming and forestry being dealt with in different ways.

The two most important pieces of planning legislation for countryside managers are the 1947 Town and Country Planning Act (which established the planning machinery) and the 1971 Town and Country Planning Act (which rationalized and updated earlier legislation). In Scotland, these pieces of legislation were reflected in comparable enactments.

Section 22 of the 1971 Act defines development as: 'the setting construction of building, engineering, mining or other operations in, on, over or under land'. For the managers of countryside recreation sites, the implications of the development control process of planning are, therefore, twofold: first, any building or earth works, for example, will require planning permission and; secondly, where a country park or estate area is being created from land previously used for another purpose this too will require planning permission from the Local Authority. Adapting an old barn to be used as a visitor centre, therefore, requires all the relevant planning approvals. The site manager should clearly seek expert planning advice before any 'development' takes place on a recreation site.

Other elements of planning and land use control functions of the law are of relevance to the manager. Development plans drawn up by the Local Authority planning department identify zones for types of development; housing, industrial, recreational and so on. This process is constantly under review and needs to adapt to accommodate demographic and other considerations. However, the manager should be aware of the most up-to-date development plans in order to place the recreational development into a wider planning framework.

When planning approval is given for development, or improvement, at countryside sites, certain conditions may be placed on the proposals. Particularly if the site is in a sensitive area (in which, by definition, many countryside recreation sites are located), this might include suitable landscaping or the use of appropriate construction materials., Even without such planning conditions, these matters are of importance to the countryside manager who must seek to protect the amenity and landscape integrity of his or her site.

8.2.2 Conservation

The British legal system for protecting and conserving the wildlife and landscape of the countryside has been assembled in a somewhat piecemeal way (Bromley, 1990). There have, however, been three broad objectives to the relevant legislation; first, to delineate and provide some protection to specific areas of land within the British Isles; secondly, to provide specific protection to named species of animals and plants; and thirdly, to empower and impose a duty on government agencies and bodies to have 'due regard for' protecting the visual, wildlife and other considerations of the natural environment.

Thus, the 1949 National Parks and Access to the Countryside Act provided the mechanism for designating National Parks and Areas of Outstanding Natural Beauty (but not in Scotland) and Sites of Special Scientific Interest. It also began to structure the information gathering process needed to identify public-rights of-way. The 1968 Countryside Act (1967 in Scotland) provided Local Authorities with the power to create country parks and laid down the formation of the Countryside Commissions for England and Wales, and Scotland and for these commissions to, amongst other things, issue grants to public, private and voluntary organizations and individuals to help them to develop countryside recreation sites, and protect the landscape. The 1981 Wildlife and Countryside Act addressed the protection of specific species of animals and plants and added further legislation to the designation of Sites of Special Scientific Interest and to the public-right-of-way network.

More recent legislation, such as the 1985 Wildlife and Countryside (Amendments) Act and the 1986 Agriculture Act, has added different types of land category and further species to the lists created since 1949.

But where does all of this leave the countryside recreation manager?

The conservation legislation has a number of implications for the manager.

First, the manager may be responsible for promoting and managing countryside recreation within one of these specialist designations. This is, however, a relatively rare situation in that much of the land given special designation remains in individual and/or private ownership, and thus outside the direct control of any single manager, although a manager may have responsibility for 'recreation' across a wide area.

Secondly, if the site manager works within a Local Authority or statutory undertaker, the law places upon the manager the duty to have due regard for a wide range of environmental considerations. Therefore, any recreational opportunities that are provided for must statutorily accommodate wider concerns. In the private sector, such a statutory duty does not exist, except through the planning system identified earlier. However, there still does exist a professional duty to protect the natural history, landscape and other facets of the countryside whilst providing for recreation.

Thirdly, specialist designations bring with them, on the one hand, tighter planning controls (in order to protect the very things that make the site special) and on the other, the possibility of financial support for work that conserves or enhances the specialist nature of the land.

Finally, the manager may be constrained in what he or she can do with the land above and beyond permitted development. The 1981 Wildlife and Countryside Act, for example, in Section 28, makes provision for the designation of Sites of Special Scientific Interest. Whilst notifying the owners of land upon which these sites fall, the relevant agencies that are responsible for designation, must provide a list of operations that cannot be undertaken on the land without prior consultation. Thus, the site manager, who manages a site which includes an SSSI will be limited in the activities that he or she can undertake or promote on that land.

The British framework of conservation legislation is based upon a number of underlying principles. The most fundamental of these principles is that of 'voluntary action': the land remains the property of the individual, and responsibility for conserving the countryside's integrity of wildlife and landscape value lies with him or her. This means that the site manager must carry this responsibility when providing for countryside recreation.

8.2.3 Occupier's responsibility

There are a large number of special responsibilities held by the occupier of land. Some of these are discussed in the next section under the general assessment of civil case law. Many responsibilities are, however, based in statute. Some of these relate to the activities undertaken on the land and are generally applicable to land owners. Thus, the Control of Pollution Act (1974) and the Clean Air Act (1956 and 1965) apply to all occupiers. There are, however, a number of statutory obligations for which the countryside site manager must have particular regard. These relate to the manager's responsibility for the safety of his or her visitors and staff.

The Occupiers Liability Act (1957) places upon the occupier of land (not necessarily the owner or title holder) the duty of care for the safety of those persons that are invited, or entitled to be on the land. In this sense, the occupier could well be the site manager, although the responsibility for duty of care can be shared by a number of people. People who are entitled to be on the land certainly include visitors who are positively encouraged or invited on to a recreation site. The duty of care is particularly difficult to unravel in the context of countryside recreation. As Harte (1985) states 'Those in charge of a piece of land who leave it unsafe are liable to anyone who was forseeably likely to suffer harm from its defective condition'. Under the summary of the purpose behind the law, it is clear that the definition of what might be considered as forseeable or defective is debatable. When people visit the countryside they may be seeking solitude, remoteness or a natural environment. Such an environment is, almost by definition, potentially dangerous. Thus, the manager must be aware of his or her liability and balance the type of resource and the likelihood of danger accordingly.

The occupiers liability is further complicated by a number of case studies which have tested the 1957 Act. Trespassers too may be afforded some protection under the Act, particularly if the individuals are children who may be unaware that they are trespassing. Similarly, what may be considered as safe for a healthy adult may not be safe for visually handicapped people or children. Section 2 of the 1957 Act states that 'Occupiers have a duty to take such care as is reasonable to see that the visitor will be reasonably safe in using the premises for the purpose for which he is invited or permitted by the occupier to be there'. The definition of 'reasonable' and 'safe' are never fixed absolutely.

In much the same way that visitors or invitees (and possibly trespassers) have a right to be 'safe' on land occupied by others, so too do people who work on that land. The Health and Safety at Work Act

(1974) imposes such a duty on the employer of staff. Whilst the manager will not necessarily be the employer (indeed this is most often the case) it will undoubtedly be part of the manager's responsibility to execute the employer's responsibility.

The Health and Safety Act, under Section 2, states that 'It shall be the duty of every employer to ensure, so far as is reasonably practical, the health, safety and welfare at work of all his employees'. Correspondingly, Section 7 of the Act lays a similar responsibility for reasonable care on the employee for his or her own safety and that of fellow employees. Thus, the Act lays the traditional duty of reasonable care on employers and employees, but with the onus being largely on the employer.

Other than these general duties of care, the 1974 Act sought to consolidate a large amount of proceeding Acts, such as the Factories Act (1961) and the Alkali etc. Works Regulation Act (1906)! The Act, therefore, gives the governing body of the Act (The Health and Safety Executive) the power to enforce very detailed site regulations. Health and safety is explored further in section 8.4.

8.2.4 Other statutory law

The foregoing discussion is far from exhaustive. There are many Acts of Parliament that have an impact upon the work of the countryside site manager. Parkes (1983) identifies over 17 areas of law which the countryside ranger/manager must be at least aware of. These range from indecent exposure or the use of firearms to theft and dumping of rubbish. Whilst many of these areas of law tend to be reactive, they are still important in the day-to-day working of the manager.

The legislative background to the public-rights-of-way network in England and Wales is equally important and will influence the decisions made by many managers. Clayden and Trevelyan (1983) give a detailed analysis of the intricacies of the relevant legislation. Within England and Wales (but not Scotland) the public-rights-of-way network is a necessary consideration in the management of land, not only because of existing rights of way but also because of presumed rights of way, dedicated routes, claimed routes and so on.

In short, therefore, the site manager must at least be aware of the maze of statutory laws that controls and directs the use of land. Some areas of law are particularly important and require more detailed consideration by the manager.

8.3 COMMON LAW

The British system of law has within it a number of areas that have not been covered by statute, but, nonetheless, lay binding responsibility upon land owners and managers. Historically, this area of law is built up from cases, the results and rulings of which create legal precedent for subsequent, similar situations. Thus, common or civil law is as important as statute law, but has been far less clearly defined through statute.

Three particular areas of law are relevant, namely: nuisance; negligence and trespass.

8.3.1 Nuisance

Nuisance is simply the interference with land in someone elses possession. This interference can be direct or indirect, and can be either by the action of an individual or group of individuals or by the action of some activity that is undertaken on the land, such as burning, or a noisy activity, for example.

The concept of nuisance is, therefore, of relevance to the site manager in two ways. First, as the manager of land, he or she wants to protect that asset against interference from others. Secondly, the manager also wants to ensure that the activities that are undertaken on the recreation site do not amount to a public or private nuisance.

As with all concerns of law, the law of nuisance is based upon what is, or may be considered as reasonable and what form the interference takes. What is reasonable on an urban fringe site, for example, may not be reasonable either in a town centre or indeed a more rural area.

Actions in nuisance are important for the land owner, in that they seek to protect the rights of the land, rather than protect individuals from harm. The concept of protecting the amenity value of land is, however, a nebulous one. Therefore, whilst it is often easy to place a value on physical damage, it is not easy to assess the loss of amenity through say, the noise of model aircraft. Thus, the most usual result of a case in nuisance is that the activity that constitutes the nuisance is stopped. Where actual harm occurs, it is therefore more usual for the case to be pursued in negligence rather than nuisance. As Harte (1985) suggests 'A nuisance action is most valuable in preventing the continuance of a harmful state of affairs'.

Public nuisance is nuisance that either results in a statute law being broken or, alternatively, in a sufficiently large and widespread group of people being affected by the action. As opposed to private nuisance, public nuisance is a crime and action is brought, usually, by the state.

8.3.2 Negligence

In summing up a famous case which laid down the foundation for the modern concept of negligence, Lord Atkin stated 'The rule that you are to love your neighbour becomes in law, you must not injure your neighbour . . . Who, then, in law is my neighbour? . . . persons who are so closely and directly affected by my act that I ought reasonably to have them in contemplation as being so affected when I am directing my mind to the acts or omissions which are called into question' (Atkin, 1932).

Negligence, therefore, is based on the principle that everyone owes a duty of care to all those whom may be affected by their behaviour – the acts or omissions identified by Lord Atkin. Anyone who fails to act in this way and does not show a reasonable duty of care, is acting in a negligent way. This would appear to be a very wide-ranging concept, and to avoid the over use of the laws of negligence, certain constraints have been imposed through subsequent case law. Thus, for example, negligence is restricted to cases that cause personal harm.

For the manager, it is evident that any number of activities that may be undertaken as part of the management of a site could well, if not managed carefully, give rise to negligent acts or omissions. These may or may not be also covered through relevant statutory laws, but even where a criminal case is not warranted, a civil case in negligence may be pursued. Where an estate worker fells a tree in a negligent manner that results in harm to the user of a public-right-of-way, the harmed person could well pursue a case in negligence.

As with nuisance, there are several forms of negligence, which have various characteristics. Professional negligence, for example, arises when a professional acts or instructs in a manner that ultimately leads to harm. This, too, is of relevance to the site manager who may himself be involved in advising on correct methods or procedures.

Criminal negligence arises where the results of the negligent act or omission result in a statutory law being broken, or a sufficiently large number of people being affected to warrant a public case being brought.

8.3.3 Trespass

The law of trespass is one of the oldest in Britain and seeks to protect landowners from 'interference with their land'. Originally, trespass covered action against persons and goods as well as land. However, the wide-ranging concepts of negligence and nuisance now provide better alternative methods of protection. Trespass, therefore, is now concerned with the unjustifiable and direct interference with another person's property. It is not a crime, despite landowners preoccupation with erecting 'Trespassers will be prosecuted' signs.

A case in trespass can be brought where harm occurs or where it does not occur. Where actual harm occurs damages that are awarded will inevitably be greater.

To the manager, the law of trespass provides a useful mechanism for controlling access into and around a site, although to bring an action in trespass should be seen as a last resort. A manager who brings action against people who stray off paths or wander into adjacent landowner's land will soon lose credibility as a supporter of countryside recreation.

8.4 HEALTH AND SAFETY

It is worth examining in some detail the responsibilities within the Health and Safety legislation. As an employer and an occupier of premises (including buildings and land) every organization has a duty to ensure the health and safety of employees, volunteers and visitors. In some cases (such as the control of substances hazardous to health) this responsibility lies unquestionably with the employer. In other cases, such as those raised under the Health and Safety at Work Act 1974, the responsibility is a joint one between staff, employers and managers.

- Understand your duties as manager under the Health and Safety at Work Act 1974.
- Ensure your premises fulfil the minimum requirements of the Offices, Shops and Railway Premises Act 1963.
- Have a written health and safety policy.
- Ensure that all relevant building and fire certificates are in order.
- Put employees liability and other insurance polices in place.
- Keep first aid and emergency procedures up-to-date for all staff and ensure that visitors and the public know of these precautions and how to enact them.
- Display all relevant and statutory notices for employees and public alike.
- Provide adequate training and information to staff and visitors to enable them to play their part in keeping the work place and countryside site safe.

Figure 8.1 Health and safety checklist – minimum adherence.

8.4.1 The duties of care

The main responsibilities of the employer are contained within the Health and Safety Act 1974, and the Occupiers Liability Acts of 1957 and 1984. In brief, the employer must provide; a safe place of work; safe means of access; a safe system of work; adequate materials; competent employees; protection from unnecessary risk of injury. Furthermore, the employer must have a health and safety policy if more than five persons

---

1. **INTRODUCTION**
   The Health and Safety at Work etc. Act 1974 requires the organization to prepare and, as often as may be appropriate, revise a written statement of its general policy with respect to the health and safety at work for its employees, and the organization and arrangements for the time being in force for carrying out the policy, and to bring the statement and any revision of it to the notice of all its employees.
   This requirement is met by the organization corporate safety policy statement by which the manager or site manager has a responsibility for the management of the safety function of his/her site/area of responsibility.

2. **DEPARTMENTAL SAFETY POLICY**
   The manager or site manager will take all reasonable steps to secure a safe working environment and safe working conditions and practices for both employees engaged in the organization's activities and any other person who may be affected by them.
   It is the intention to prevent, so far is as reasonably practical, injuries to any person as a result of his/her operations by the provision of safe plant and premises and the effective management of the work activities over which he/she exercises control. To this end, the manager will make available such information, training and supervision for the organization's employees as is considered necessary and will provide adequate safety devices and protective equipment for those at risk.
   Without detracting from the primary responsibility of managers and supervisors for ensuring safe conditions at work, the organization will provide advice on safety and health matters, normally through the manager or site manager, to assist line management in its task.
   The manager recognizes that a safety policy will only be successful if it actively involves all employees. He/she will, therefore, cooperate fully in the appointment of safety representatives by recognized Trade Unions and, in discussions with them, promote and develop measures to ensure adequate standards for health and safety at work.
   For their part, it is the duty of all staff under the Health and Safety etc. Act 1974 to take all reasonable care for the health and safety of themselves and their fellow employees, all third parties who may be affected by their actions at work, and to cooperate with management to enable the manager to meet his/her responsibilities.
   This statement of policy will be kept under review and any amendments to it will be brought to the notice of all employees.

Figure 8.2 General health and safety policy.

are employed by the organization (this policy will be supported by site/building/job specific codes of conduct) and the employer must provide adequate training and instruction.

For their part, the employees must also exercise their responsibility of care: this includes; taking reasonable care of the health and safety of other people (employees, volunteers or visitors) who may be affected by their acts; cooperating with their employer/manager to take steps to improve health and safety standards.

8.4.2 The management of premises

The Offices, Shops and Railway Premises Act (1963) lists a set of requirements that must be met in any place of work. These requirements include limits on minimum temperatures, minimum work space per individual, provision of sanitary washing facilities and conveniences, provision of first aid boxes and trained staff, registration of the office and guidelines for building safety. Similar regulations exist for fire precautions and other areas of building management.

It is evident, therefore, that not only does the manager have a statutory responsibility towards his or her staff, but this responsibility will extend to visitors and, in some cases, contractors.

Unlike the requirements of the Health and Safety at Work Act, certain regulations within the Offices, Shops etc. Act and other associated legislation do not automatically apply to buildings used by the public (such as minimum temperatures or spacial requirements). Some clearly do (such as provision of first aid facilities) but there do remain some areas covered by interpretation of the law rather than strict guidance.

Where the 'premises' being managed are outside, i.e. actually in the countryside, the Offices, Shops and Railway Premises Act does not apply in total, but the overriding responsibility for a safe working environment still holds.

8.4.3 COSHH

The Control of Substances Hazardous to Health Regulations (1988), and Act (1989) referred to as COSHH, place a personal duty on employers to make 'a suitable and sufficient assessment' of the risks created by employees' possible exposure to hazardous substances. As with many health and safety regulations and law, this duty extends to contractors and members of the public. The full list of hazardous substances is produced through the 'approved list' (the Classification, Packaging and Labelling of Dangerous Substances Regulations, 1989).

The significance of COSHH is that it introduces to the manager a very specific set of circumstances which involve known or named substances, and which could potentially create risk and some danger in the work place. It is a very precise element of general health and safety legislation.

The assessment of risk is carried out in three stages: identification; evaluation; control. The guidelines for managing COSHH, the responsibility for which lies with the employer, can be obtained from the Health and Safety Executive. It is safe to say, however, that the approved list contains substances ranging from glue and typewriter fluid to herbicides and acid. Thus, it is a very important and significant area of responsibility for any manager.

---

1. Identify all substances:
   - What form? Gas, liquid, solids, etc.
   - Route? Inhale, touch, splashing, etc.
   - Rating? Look at label, further information, etc.
2. Evaluate the risk:
   - Who is exposed?
   - How often?
   - How many?
   - How much?
3. How can exposure be controlled:
   - Elimination or substitution;
   - Reduction by ventilation, work practice or hygiene;
   - Protection, by clothing or equipment;
   - Control of storage and disposal.

Figure 8.3 Assessment of hazard under COSHH.

8.5 SUMMARY

Common law is a complex web of case law, which itself is often based upon historic, legal precedents. To the manager the law provides both a means of protecting his or her concern and a mechanism that protects the public from negligent or other acts by the manager or his or her staff. It is, therefore, almost unnecessary to emphasize that the manager cannot be expected to understand fully the whole legal framework within which he or she operates. Thus, professional legal advice is vital for the important stages of site development and management. The manager must, however, at the very least, be aware of the complexities and inferences of the law. In the words of the famous legal maxim 'Ignorantia juris non excusat' – ignorance of the law is no excuse.

Other issues | 9

9.1 INTRODUCTION

The countryside recreation site offers many different experiences and seeks to meet many objectives. These objectives cover a variety of themes: recreation provision, landscape protection, natural history conservation and, not least, operating within the law! These issues have all been discussed in the preceding pages. The fact that a balance has to be struck between potentially conflicting interests indicates that the development and management of a countryside recreation site amounts to more than simply combining a number of land uses on any particular site. The resultant balance has to be continually monitored, controlled and directed. That is the primary function of management. Rather than summarize the foregoing chapters, therefore, this concluding chapter will look at the other elements of this balancing act, at some of the future influences on this process, and, finally at some brief examples of how various sites are managed.

9.2 THE ROLE OF THE MANAGER

The manager of countryside recreation sites must, like all managers, have command of a number of areas of expertise. These are summarized in Figure 9.1. Other than knowledge of the environment, the manager of a countryside recreation site will clearly need knowledge of the recreational process and how to manage personnel, internal procedures and so on – what the Countryside Staff Training Advisory Group (CSTAG) (1989) refers to as managing the system. This book has concentrated upon elements of managing the environment and of recreational management. There is some benefit, therefore, in further assessing the management of recreation and of managing the system.

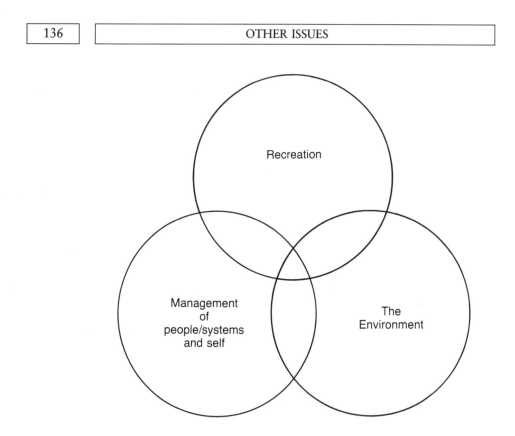

Figure 9.1 Skills required by the manager.

9.2.1 Recreation management

The Yates Report (Recreation Management Training Committee, 1984) placed the management of countryside recreation sites clearly within the overall context of recreational management. The report, therefore, concluded that managers of countryside facilities had similar training needs to those of other recreation managers. There is clearly a lot to be gained by understanding the overall recreation and leisure process; why do people seek recreational outlets; what are the barriers to recreation; what types of people visit the countryside as opposed to say, the theatre; are all questions that form part of the leisure environment within which countryside sites operate, and at a purely commercial level, financial success will depend upon 'competing' with other leisure and recreational opportunities in an area. Torkildsen (1986) provides a comprehensive overview of the leisure industry and management within the industry. Whilst few managers of countryside recreation sites would accept that recreation provision is their sole concern, few would disagree that knowledge of the wider recreational culture is a necessary prerequisite of effective management.

9.2.2 Managing the system

Management is, in itself, a skill, and, therefore, needs to be understood, practised and developed. Furthermore, each organization also has its own particular (and often peculiar) management culture. Countryside recreation sites operate as part of this culture and thus the manager needs to develop the necessary skills in 'system management'. A charitable trust, such as a county conservation trust, operates in a different way to a Local Authority, for example. These differences will be reflected in the aims and objectives of the management plan and the people to whom a site manager is responsible, in the way that the organization is structured and decisions are made. The manager of a countryside recreation site will need to develop the necessary management skills to operate in these situations.

Management as a specialist subject has been the topic of many studies and research. The manager of a countryside recreation site will normally be too preoccupied managing the 'countryside' and the 'recreation' to devote very much time to studying the processes of management. Therefore, the manager must be prepared to develop management expertise within the context of the environmental work. For this reason, on-the-job training is usually most appropriate, with personal development, as promoted by Young (1986), being relevant.

The foregoing discussion is designed to do no more than identify the breadth of understanding that is involved in managing the countryside recreation site.

Other than the immediate system within which the site operates, numerous other factors influence and constrain the management of the site. These external influences include the national Town and Country planning systems, political trends, population and leisure patterns and, increasingly, international legislation and pressures. These external factors are clearly beyond the immediate control of the manager, yet they have a major effect on the provision of countryside recreation sites. Furthermore, the externalities are continually changing and must, therefore, be understood. The following section deals with some of the factors which are likely to influence the provision, popularity and design of countryside recreation sites into the early part of the 21st century.

9.3 EXTERNAL FACTORS

The number of factors that influence countryside recreation provision is almost endless; indeed almost anything can be considered to be of influence, ranging from the price of petrol to the length of the average working week. However, four general areas can be identified which are of significant importance, these are: legislation, especially that generated through the European Community: the trends within environmental recreation; the growth of the leisure industry; changes that are occurring in environmental awareness.

9.3.1 Legislation

The legal framework that surrounds the operations of a countryside recreation site is covered in Chapter 8. Increasingly, however, the legal framework for the environment is being determined, or at least broadly defined, through European legislation and directives. The Commission of European Communities (1988) identifies the general policy framework for European environmental legislation. The main thrust of the legislation is towards nature conservation both at a species level and an area level. The impact of this upon countryside recreation will be tighter control on the management of the natural environment or, more specifically, Environmental Impact Assessments will be required more often for development within the countryside (Department of the Environment, 1988). Therefore, recreation sites will need to be evermore sympathetic to the landscape and natural history requirements of the countryside. Whether or not a formal Environmental Impact Assessment is required from the developer, it should be considered an integral element of the process of management planning to incorporate the wider impact of the site on, for example, visibility horizons, increased traffic flows, run-off or other effects on neighbouring habitats and the on-site damage caused by increased visitor numbers.

There exists in Britain a network of specially designated landscapes and natural habitats (National Parks, National Scenic Areas in Scotland, Sites of Special Scientific Interest and Areas of Outstanding Natural Beauty, for example). Whilst this broad network will not change dramatically, the controls on development in the countryside will be increasingly towards maintaining the natural integrity of the countryside, whilst at the same time encouraging economic diversity (Department of the Environment, 1989). Thus, for the private sector, for example, the well-designed recreation site will represent an addition to the traditional primary-based industry of rural areas.

9.3.2 Leisure trends

The concept of the theme park, like the concept of National Parks, and countryside rangers, was borrowed from the USA. The 'theme' concept is now well entrenched in many types of leisure provision, and is increasingly becoming accepted in areas that formerly were never seen (or more strictly, never saw themselves) as part of the leisure industry, such as museums (O'Halloran, 1989). In a theme park, be it in the urban setting or in the countryside, the recreational element is foremost, with some consideration being given to education and interpretation through the theme of the park. For the manager of a countryside recreation site, the idea of a theme is necessary to help interpret a site and to pitch the education at a level that can be easily understood. However, to take the theme concept too far would jeopardize the other considerations that need to be taken into account – landscape quality, natural history and educational quality. Fieldhouse (1989) asked 'Could the whole of the land be turned into a large leisure park, with no agricultural holdings except in rare breeds corrals? That certainly will destroy the delicately balanced landscape pattern'.

9.3.3 The leisure boom

Dower (1965) was one of the first people to articulate both the opportunities and the problems to be faced by the growth in demand for leisure pursuits. Since then, the demand for leisure activity in Britain has shown no signs of diminishing. There is no doubt that the activities that are sought by recreationalists or the opportunities that are provided by managers have changed significantly over the decades. The leisure industry now includes museums, sports halls, home-based videos, do-it-yourself improvements and shopping. The new age of leisure is continually upon us (Delaney, 1990, for example). The message for all managers of leisure facilities – and this includes the providers of countryside recreation sites – is that for the foreseeable future, recreation will be part of a larger industry. Where boundaries are drawn within this industry will change, but Stewart (1989) suggests that for the late 1990s and early 21st century 'leisure is the way forward'.

9.3.4 Environmental awareness

It is regularly suggested that in the latter part of the 20th century, the various strands of concern for the environment which had manifested themselves in various ways throughout the century began to come together. Thus, access lobby groups and landscape protection groups (as well as more latterly, antipollution campaigners and a myriad of community-based pressure groups) all came to see themselves as part of a larger 'environmental' movement. In the political arena, this has given rise to the Green Politics of Europe (Porritt, 1984).

For the manager of a countryside recreation site, this cohesion within the environmental movement will mean that the role of the countryside site and the manager may change. First, the desire for more knowledge is likely to increase – not just about the particular site, but also about the links between the site and wider environmental issues. Secondly, the generally rising levels of environmental awareness will inevitably give rise to higher levels of recreational demand in countryside areas and, more subjectively, will make greater demands upon the skills of the manager to provide an attractive and environmentally sustainable site to a more aware group of visitors.

9.4 PUTTING THE PIECES TOGETHER

It is stressed throughout this book that the role of the manager is crucial in balancing the requirements of the environment, those of the visitors and recreationalists, and the constraints of the professional system within which he or she operates. These requirements and constraints will be influenced by and, in return influence, the decisions of the manager and his or her staff. In order to understand the dialogue, it is necessary to study the way that certain types of countryside recreation sites are managed, and how they operate. This is clearly a practical exercise, which cannot be recorded in a satisfactory manner here. A list of the types of facilities that might be provided and the types of organizations that may develop and manage them will give some indication of the scope of the opportunities for countryside recreation.

The private sector provides a range of countryside recreation sites, from country estates, perhaps catering for specific types of recreation, such as angling or horse riding to more open, informal provision of open farms or picnic areas in association with museums or other theme-type attractions. Inevitably, in order to survive in the economic environment, as well as the natural environment, some form of income generation is necessary. However, Robinson (1984) suggests 'that income generation and conservation are not mutually exclusive and people who believe that this is automatically true, are in cloud cuckoo land'.

The voluntary sector provide many countryside recreation sites. The National Trust, which in 1990 had almost 2 million members, owns many countryside areas, which provide differing levels of managed recreational opportunities. Local county-based conservation trusts, on the other hand, exist primarily to protect specific site-based areas of natural history importance. However, these sites will invariably have some recreational interest, if only for the members of the trusts, and this element will need to be, at the very least, acknowledged within the management process.

Finally, the public sector provides many country parks, picnic sites and project/access areas all of which have recreational enjoyment as one of their principal objectives. Along with their wider statutory obligations, Local Authorities (County and District Authorities, and Metropolitan Authorities in England and Wales and Regional and District Authorities in Scotland) can provide a range of recreational facilities, including countryside-based areas. Similarly, other government organizations such as the Forestry Commission are not only obliged to protect and improve the natural environment, but also provide recreational opportunities for the public. This can be no more than a car-park and some picnic tables, or can be a visitor centre, with associated trails, walks, exhibition and educational programmes.

The common thread that links all of these types of facility is the need for a comprehensive management plan and, where necessary, a business plan to ensure the proper balance of all the resources at the manager's disposal.

9.5 SUMMARY

This handbook has only been able to outline the basic management considerations for countryside recreation sites. However, even through this necessarily brief analysis, it is clear that the manager requires a broad understanding of a wide range of skills; legal, professional, environmental, educational and so on. Within this spectrum, each manager will have his or her own areas of expertise and will have strengths and, just as importantly, weaknesses. In this context, individual managers will need to be responsible for much of their own development. At a practical level this book offers an assessment of the areas within which the manager needs some degree of expertise. It also offers a framework – the management plan – within which this expertise can be brought to bear, to the benefits of the site and the visitor alike. In this way, it is to be hoped, the future of the countryside can be ensured which in turn will ensure that people can continue to enjoy its beauty.

And since to look at things in bloom,
Fifty springs are little room,
About the woodlands I will go,
To see the cherry hung with snow.

A. E. Houseman

Bibliography

Aldridge, D. (1975) *A Guide to Countryside Interpretation: Part 1*, HMSO, Edinburgh.

Atkin, Lord (1932) *Donoghue v Stevenson*, A C 562 HL.

Barber, A. (1991) *A Guide to Management Plans for Parks and Open Spaces*, Institute for Leisure and Amenity Management, Reading.

Barrow, G. (1988) *Vistor Centres: An Introduction in Environmental Interpretation*, Centre for Environmental Interpretation, Manchester.

Barrow, C. and Barrow, P. (1990) *Business Plan Workbook*, Kogan Page, London.

Blunden, J. and Curry, N. (1988) *A Future for our Countryside*, Blackwell Scientific Publications, London.

British Travel Association (1967) *Pilot National Recreation Survey*, University of Keele, Keele.

British Trust for Conservation Volunteers (Various) *Handbooks on: Hedging; Footpaths; Waterways; Walls; Fencing*, BTVC, Wallingford.

Bromley, P. (1990) *Countryside Management*, E & FN Spon, London.

Campbell, A. (1987) *The Designer's Handbook*, Orbis Books, London.

Centre for Environmental Interpretation (1987) *Focus on Living History*, CEI, Manchester.

Centre for Leisure Research (1986) *Access Study Summary Report*, CCP 216, Countryside Commission/Sports Council, Cheltenham.

Clamp, H. (1989) *Landscape Professional Practice*, Gower Press, Guildford.

Clawson, M. and Knetsch, J. L. (1966) *The Economics of Outdoor Recreation*, John Hopkins Press, Baltimore.

Clay, R. (1984) *Marketing: The Introduction to a Concept*, Coventry Leisure Services, Seminar Proceedings.

Clayden, P. and Trevelyan J. (1983) *Rights of Way: A Guide to Law and Practice*, Ramblers Association, London.

Commission of European Communities (1988) *European Community Environment Legislation, Vol. 1*, CEC, Brussels.

Coppock, J. T. and Duffield, B. S. (1975) *Recreation in the Countryside*, Macmillan Press, London.

Countryside Commission (1974) *Farm Open Days*, CCP 77, Cheltenham.

Countryside Commission (1976) *The Bollin Valley*, CCP 97, Cheltenham.

Countryside Commission (1979a) *Interpretive Planning*. Advisory Series No. 2, Cheltenham.

Countryside Commission (1979b) *Countryside Rangers and Related Staff*. Advisory Series No. 7, Cheltenham.

Countryside Commission (1980a) *Recreational Cycling*. Advisory Series No. 8, Cheltenham.

Countryside Commission (1980b) *Volunteers in the Countryside*. Advisory Series No. 11, Cheltenham.

Countryside Commission (1980c) *Audio-visual Media in Countryside Interpretation*. Advisory Series No. 12, Cheltenham.

Countryside Commission (1981) *Informal Countryside Recreation for Disabled People*. Advisory Series No. 14, Cheltenham.

Countryside Commission (1984) *A Strategy for Hadrians Wall*, Cheltenham.

Countryside Commission (1985a) *Country Park Visitor Surveys*, CCP 180, Cheltenham.

Countryside Commission (1985b) *Cannock Chase: 1979–1984. A Country Park Plan on Trial*, CCP 181, Cheltenham.

Countryside Commission (1985c) *National Countryside Recreation Survey*, CCP 201, Cheltenham.

Countryside Commission (1986) *An Assessment of Amenity Tree Planting Schemes*. Occasional Papers Series, Cheltenham.

Countryside Commission (1987a) *Planning for Countryside in Metropolitan Areas*, CCP 224, Cheltenham.

Countryside Commission (1987b) *Enjoying the Countryside*, CCP 225, Cheltenham.

Countryside Commission (1988) *Landscape Assessment of Farm Land*, CCP 255, Cheltenham.

Countryside Commission (1989) *Managing Rights of Way: an Agenda for Action*, CCP 273, Cheltenham.

Countryside Commission (1991) *Caring for the Countryside*, CCP 351, Cheltenham.

Countryside Commission for Scotland (1981) *Display Sheets and Information*, Bettleby, Perth.

Countryside Commission for Scotland (1984) *Childrens Play in the Countryside*, Battleby, Perth.

Countryside Policy Review Panel (1987) *New Opportunities for the Countryside*, CCP 224, Cheltenham.

Countryside Staff Training Advisory Group (1989) *Training for Tomorrow's Countryside*. CSTAG Report, Countryside Commission, Cheltenham.

Craig, S. (1989) *Marketing Leisure Services*, Leisure Futures Ltd, London.

Croners (1991) *Croners Guide to Personnel Management*, Croners, London.

Cullingworth, D. (1970) *An Outline of Planning Law*, Sweet and Maxwell, London.

Curry, N. R. (1991) *Countryside Recreation*, E & FN Spon, London.

Delaney, J. (1990) Marketing the new age of leisure. *Leisure Manager*, **2** (January), 54–6.

Department of Employment (1957) *Occupiers Liability Act*, HMSO, London.

Department of Employment (1979) *Health and Safety at Work Act*, HMSO, London.

Department of the Environment (1947) *Town and Country Planning Act*, HMSO, London.

Department of the Environment (1949) *National Parks and Access to the Countryside Act*, HMSO, London.

Department of the Environment (1967) *Countryside Act (Scotland)*, HMSO, London.

Department of the Environment (1968) *Countryside Act*, HMSO, London.

Department of the Environment (1981) *Wildlife and Countryside Act*, HMSO, London.

Department of the Environment (1985) *Wildlife and Countryside (Amendments) Act*, HMSO, London.

Department of the Environment (1988) *Environmental Assessment Circular 15/88*, HMSO, London.

Department of the Environment (1989) *Planning Guidelines; Countryside and Rural Economy*, HMSO, London.

Department of the Environment (1990) *Environmental Protection Act*, HMSO, London.

Department of the Environment (1992) *Fit for the Future: A Statement by the Government on Policies for the National Parks*, HMSO, London.

Dower, J. (1965) *Leisure: The Fourth Wave*, Civic Trust, London.

Duffield, B. S. and Owen, M. L. (1970) *Leisure and Countryside: A Geographical Appraisal of Countryside Recreation in Lanarkshire*, University of Edinburgh.

Dyke, J. (1986) Introduction to self-guide trails, *Environmental Interpretation*, November, 4–6.

Elson, M. (1992) Green Belts: A symbol of Green Planning, *Landscape Design*, February, 10–13.

English Heritage (1980) *Visitors Welcome*, Centre for Environmental Interpretation, Manchester.

Fieldhouse, K. (1989) Land's End: An Experience to Remember?, *Landscape Design*, July, 17–21.

Forester, S. (1989) *Environmental Grants*, Directory of Social Change, London.

Glyplis, S. (1991) *Countryside Recreation*, Longmans, London.

Greenstreet, R. (1980) *Legal and Contractual Procedures for Architects*, Architects Journal Press, London.

Haigh, N. (1987) *EEC Environmental Policy and Britain*, Longman, Harlow.

Hall, P. (1975) *Urban and Regional Planning*, Pelican, Harmondsworth.

Hart, R. A. (1979) *Childrens Experience of Space*, Irvington Press, New York.

Harte, J. D. C. (1985) *Landscape, Land-use and the Law*, E & FN Spon, London.

Heap, D. (1973) *An Outline of Planning Law*, Sweet and Maxwell, London.

Henry, I. (1983) Marketing objectives in public sector marketing, *Leisure Management*, **6** (November), 7–12.

Hudson, M. (1978) *The Bicycle Planning Book*, Friends of the Earth, London.

Kodak (1976) *Understanding Sound and Video Recording*, Lutterworth Press, London.

Kotler, P. (1975) *Marketing for a Non-Profit Organisation*, Prentice-Hall, New Jersey.

Kraus, R. (1978) *Recreation and Leisure in Modern Society*, Goodyear Press, California.

Leay, A. Rowe, J. and Young, J. D. (1986) *Management Plans: A Guide to their Preparations and Use*, Countryside Commission, Cheltenham.

Lindesay, W. (1985) A review of outdoor interpretive panels, *Environmental Interpretation*, June, 2–7.

Lowe, P. D. and Goyder, J. (1983) *Environmental Groups in Politics*, George Allen and Unwin, London.

Melhulish, P. (1987) *Young National Trust Theatre, Living History*, Centre for Environmental Interpretation, Manchester.

Miles, C. W. N. and Seabrooke, W. (1993) *Recreation Land Management*, E & FN Spon, London.

Ministry of Agriculture (1986) *Agriculture Act*, HMSO, London.

Nature Conservancy Council (1983) *A Handbook for the Preparation of Management Plans*, NCC, Peterborough.

Nature Conservancy Council (1987) *Annual Report*, NCC, Peterborough.

Nature Conservancy Council (1988) *Tyne and Wear Nature Conservation Strategy*, NCC, Peterborough.

Nottinghamshire County Council (1983) *Visitor Surveys at Sherwood Forest and Rufford Country Park*, SCPR, Nottingham.

O'Halloren, M. (1989) Clerkenwell crusade, *Leisure News*, **12**, 32.

Open University (1985) *The Changing Countryside*, Croom Helm, London.

Overman, M. (1977) *Understanding Sound and Video Recordings*, Lutterworth Press, London.

Parkes, C. (1983) *Laws of the Countryside*, Association of Countryside Rangers, Suffolk.

Patmore, A. (1972) *Land and Leisure*, Penguin Books, Harmondsworth.

Pennyfather, K. (1975) *Guide to Countryside Interpretation, Part 2*, HMSO, Edinburgh.

Piersenne, A. (1985) Planning, scripting and siting panels, *Environmental Intrepretation*, June, 8–11.

Porritt, J. (1984) *Seeing Green*, Blackwell Scientific Publications, London.

Rayston, K. (1985) Countryside, sport and leisure – private estates, in *Countryside, Leisure and Jobs*, Countryside and Recreation Research Advisory Group Report, CRRAG, Bristol.

Recreation Management Training Committee (1984) *The Yates Committee. Final Report*, Department of the Environment, HMSO, London.

Robinson, K. (1984) *The private sector*, in *Training in the Countryside*, Countryside and Recreation Research Advisory Group Annual Report, CRRAG, Bristol.

Robinson, T. W. (1979) *Exmoor National Park Interpretive Plan*, Countryside Commission, Cheltenham.

Rogers, A. *et al.* (1985) *The Countryside Handbook*, Croom Helm, London.

Sayers, P. (1990) *Grounds Maintenance: A Guide to Compulsory Competitive Tendering*, E & FN Spon, London.

Sharpe, G. W. (1976) *Interpreting the Environment*, John Wiley, New York.

Shell UK (1986) *Raising Money for Environmental Improvements: Shell Better Britain Campaign*, Nature Conservancy Council, Peterborough.

Sidaway, R. (1991) *Good Conservation Practice for Sports and Recreation*, Sports Council, London.

Sports Council (1988) *Sport in the Community: A Strategy for Sport*, Sports Council, London.

Stewart, C. (1989) The leading edge, *Leisure News*, 3 (November), 30–3.

Tait, J., Lane, A. and Carr, S. (1988) *Enjoying the Countryside*, CCP 235, Cheltenham.

Tilden, F. (1967) *Interpreting our Heritage*, University of North Carolina Press, Chapel Hill.

Torkildsen, G. (1986) *Leisure and Recreation Management*, E & FN Spon, London.

Tourism and Recreation Research Unit (1980) *A Study of Four Parks around Glasgow*, TRRU Report 44, Edinburgh.

Tourism and Recreation Research Unit (1983) *Recreation Site Survey Manual*, TRRU, Edinburgh.

Turner, J. (1988) The Lee Valley: an assessment, *Landscape Design*, 172 (April).

United States National Park Service (1975) *Tatton Park Interpretive Plan*, Cheshire County Council, Chester.

Van Matre, S. (1972) *Acclimatization: A Sensory and Conceptual Approach to Ecological Involvement*, American Camping Association, Indiana.

Vasey, T. (1985) Planning and interpretive publication, *Environmental Interpretation*, Centre for Environmental Interpretation, Manchester.

Vaughan, R. (1988) *Marketing and Countryside Recreation*, University of Sussex, Brighton.

Wakefield Groundwork Trust (1989) *Annual Report*, Wakefield Groundwork Trust, Wakefield.

Westmacott, R. and Worthington, T. (1975) *Shipley Country Park Farm Interpretation Plan*, Countryside Commission, Cheltenham.

West Midlands County Council (1984) *A Nature Conservation Strategy for the County of West Midlands*, WMCC, Birmingham.

Wilkinson, J. (1985) *A Step in the Right Direction: Marketing Circular Walks*, Sports Council, London.

Wood, J. B. and Warren, A. (1978) *A Handbook for the Preparation of Management Plans*, University College, London.

Young, A. (1986) *The Manager's Handbook*, Sphere Books, London.

Index